SALONICA
and Northern Greece

By the staff of Berlitz Guides

How to use our guide

- All the practical information, hints and tips that you will need before and during the trip start on page 98, with a complete rundown of contents on page 101.

- For general background, see the sections The Region and the People, p. 6, and A Brief History, p. 12.

- All the sights to see are listed between pages 24 and 79. Our own choice of sights most highly recommended is pinpointed by the Berlitz traveller symbol.

- Entertainment, nightlife and all other leisure activities are described from pages 79 to 91, while information on restaurants and cuisine is to be found between pages 91 and 97.

- Finally, there is an index at the back of the book, pp. 126–128.

Although we make every effort to ensure the accuracy of all the information in this book, changes occur incessantly. We cannot therefore take responsibility for facts, prices, addresses and circumstances in general that are constantly subject to alteration. Our guides are updated on a regular basis as we reprint, and we are always grateful to readers who let us know of any errors, changes or serious omissions they come across.

Text: Catherine McLeod
Photography: Jean-Claude Vieillefond
Drawings: Aude Aquoise
We wish to thank the Greek National Tourist Organization, especially Frixos P. Mandamadiotis and Michael George Petropolos. We are also grateful to Vicky Nicolopoulou, Jan Pierce and Gareth Trewartha for their help in the preparation of this guide.

4 Cartography: Falk-Verlag, Hamburg

Contents

Maps

Cover picture: Mount Áthos
Photo pp. 2–3: Salonica's acropolis

5

The Region and the People

Northern Greece is full of contrasts—sun and sand, mountains and plains, olives and apricots—but not yet too full of tourists. They are just beginning to discover the beauty and riches of a region Alexander the Great knew well. Beach after glorious beach is washed by the warm Aegean, and there are mountains too. Wide plains

stretch to the horizon and historic pillars rise under a sky of legendary blue.

This big land has space enough for the good life. New international resorts have added the unmistakable tang of sophistication to the scent of pine and salt. Sleek yachts find moorings in the specially constructed harbour at Pórto Carrás. Fine food and wines grace the tables of luxury hotels.

The region extends from the Grámmos mountains, which mark the Albanian border, to the River Évros, the dividing line between Greece and Turkey. It runs north to Yugoslavia and Bulgaria and forms part of the historic Balkans. The Via Egnatia, the great Roman military road between the Adriatic and Byzantium, passed through here, and the main modern highway east still largely follows the course of the Roman road.

In the centre are the rich grainlands of the province of Macedonia, territory that formed the nucleus of a powerful ancient kingdom. Across the River Néstos is the province of Thrace and its tobacco plantations, wheeling sunflowers and ox-drawn carts.

Holiday-makers are attracted by the lure of Halkidiki, a piece of land that juts from the mainland like an outstretched hand, extending three fingers into the sea. The western coast and two of the peninsulas offer some of the most splendid beaches in Greece.

First comes Kassándra, 150 miles of developed coastline with a choice of all grades of hotels, excellent campsites and private accommodation. Sitho-nía, the middle peninsula, is more rugged, steep and pine-laden. Sandy, crescent-shaped beaches, coves and inlets can be yours alone here. Mount Áthos, the holy and largely inaccessible third peninsula, is a monastic republic of the Greek Orthodox Church. The mountain that gives the repub-lic its name rises lofty and

Colourful costumes for festive occasions and beautiful beaches like Makriámmos on Thásos island are part of the northern Greek scene.

snow-capped, bluish with mist and vegetation.

Two islands, the mysterious Samothrace and lush Thásos, are contrasting jewels suspended from the coast. The first is pebbly and scantily populated, filled with the sound of goat bells and haunted by memories of rites to the Great Gods. Thásos seems to have compressed into one island all that is loveliest in Greece—clear light, sandy beaches, generous springs, bright boats and villages, plane trees, wild flowers and the graceful remains of an old culture. In addition there are good roads and a plentiful choice of accommodation.

The capital of Northern Greece is the port city of Salo-

Some of Salonica's old houses still survive near the acropolis.

nica. Second only to Athens in size, Salonica is as modern as concrete, plate-glass and thriving commerce can make it. Yet the town has a past as old as that of Byzantium itself, and some of the gilded dust from that stronghold of Eastern Christianity still powders it.

Macedonia and Thrace are rich in history. When you tire of the beaches and need a break from snorkelling and sunning, you can follow in the footsteps of Alexander the Great or trace the more gentle itinerary of Saint Paul. Archae-

Boats and fishing remain inherent to the Greek way of life. At Pórto Koufó everything has to be made ready for the real work of the night.

ologists have discovered Alexander's capital of Pélla, boasting beautiful mosaic floors of pale river pebbles, some 20 miles north-west of Salonica. When the Kingdom of Macedonia was at the height of its glory, Alexander set out from here to cross the Hellespont and begin conquest of the known world. In Philippi Saint Paul baptized the first Macedonian convert to Christianity, a woman named Lydia, and European history entered a new epoch.

Near the town of Petrálona, twisted stalagmite columns divide a vast cave where traces of early man have been found. Aristotle was born in Stágira, one of the villages of northern

Mount Fengári in Samothrace, a lofty ringside seat, to watch the siege of Troy. Thásos was colonized at the command of the Delphic oracle.

Northern Greece draws the sportsman. There is the lure of fishing and hunting from mid-September to March in the hillier, more forested areas rich in partridge, wild pig and rabbit. No sign remains of the lions which once gave the Persians an uneasy time in Macedonia, although their existence is confirmed by Pélla's superb mosaic of a lion hunt. You are not likely to run across a jackal, but there are huge colonies of herons for the birdwatcher. Tortoises, which seem older than the gods, make thoughtful progress along the roadsides.

In Macedonia and Thrace you'll find all the attractions of Greece: climate, water sports, picturesque fishing ports, archaeological sites, Byzantine churches and new friends to be made. Here the famous *bouzoúki* evening is likely to be a spontaneous village affair, with outsiders expected to join in as a matter of course. All you need to do is choose your centre of operations, perhaps on one of Halkidiki's beaches or in Salonica itself, and from there begin your discovery of this beautiful and historic region.

Halkidiki. The rattle of wheat stalks in the fields of Macedonia and Thrace recalls the clash of warring swords. Peoples have come and gone—Persians, Bulgars, Serbs, Goths, Romans, Turks.

Greece being Greece, the gods made their presence felt from time to time. After all, Mount Olympus, their traditional home, marks the division between Macedonia and the neighbouring province of Thessaly. Poseidon sat on

11

A Brief History

Northern Greece had a different, rather slower development than the southern area, until the two joined and formed the prodigious civilization we know. The first inhabitants of Macedonia probably lived on the Halkidiki peninsula, occupying caves like the one at Petrálona, which gave its name to a Neanderthal-type skull found here—the *archanthropus europaeus petraloniensis*. It is estimated to be at least 50,000 years old.

In Neolithic times, hunting and fishing gave way to an agricultural existence. Indications of an ancient farming settlement have been discovered near Véria at Néa Nikomídia.

Northern Greece

Much of the information given below is contained in different sections of our guide, but for your convenience, key facts are grouped together here for a quick briefing.

Compare them with these figures for Greece as a whole: *surface* 50,547 square miles; *coastline* 9,385 miles; *population* approx. 10,000,000.

Geography   Northern Greece comprises the provinces of Macedonia and Thrace. Covers 16,454 square miles with 800 miles of coastline. *Population:* 2,470,000. *Capital:* Salonica (816,000). *Climate:* mild winters, sub-tropical summers, 300 days of sunshine.

Government   Hellenic Republic proclaimed June 1, 1973. Parliament elected November 17, 1974. North divided into two administrative districts headed by local governors.

Religion   Greek Orthodox church officially recognized. Established during Byzantine period when Christianity developed two centres, one in Rome, the other in Constantinople. Headed by Patriarch of Constantinople and Archbishop of Athens. *Membership:* 96% of all Greeks.

Getting around   Bus, train, car, taxi, ferry. Hired car most convenient. Taxis plentiful and inexpensive in Salonica. Travelling is mostly on foot on Mount Áthos. *Approximate distances:* Salonica–Alexandroúpolis 340 kilometres; Salonica–Kavála 165 kilometres.

According to myth, its inhabitants were descended from Pelasgos, who taught his people to wear pigs' skins, build huts and eat acorns.

The southward migration of Indo-Germanic tribes, including the Achaeans, Aeolians, Ionians and Dorians, began in about 2000 B.C. Some of them travelled as far as the southernmost end of the Greek peninsula. Historians have named all of them Hellenes.

A Macedonian Monarchy

Northern Greece failed to keep up with the great civilizations that flourished in the south. The area was still largely populated by various tribes, no longer "barbarian" (a term accorded by the Greeks to all foreigners), but not quite Greek either, who were gradually assimilated into the population. They peppered their speech with strange foreign words and constructions, and were more or less held together by kings. Perdikkas established a kingdom at Aegae and was the first of the Macedonian monarchs. Northern court circles retained their independence, maintaining economic and military links with the south. But after the 6th century B.C., Hellenic influence from the south became stronger.

Persian Wars

The rise of Hellenism was challenged by the expansion of Persia. The two powers came into conflict when Athens assisted the revolt of Greeks in Asia Minor under Persian control. Retaliation by Persia was speedy, but unsuccessful. A storm off Mount Áthos sank a fleet on its way to Attica in 492 B.C. Persian forces were defeated at Marathon two years later, then in the Bay of Salamis in 480 B.C. The decisive battle took place in 479 B.C. at Plataea. The Persians were soundly beaten and Greek independence was preserved, making possible the achievements of the 5th century.

The Golden Age

Greece's golden 5th century was the time of Pericles and the erection of the beautiful buildings which crown the Athenian acropolis. It was an era when great men like Socrates and Plato assembled in Athens. The north was not cut off from this. King Archelaus (ruled 413–399 B.C.) was a patron of the arts and the new Macedonian capital of Pélla welcomed such personalities as the painter Zeuxis, the poet Agathon and the dramatist Euripides. Archelaus was noted for his **13** road-building (the Via Egnatia later incorporated some of his routes) and, above all, for his palace. According to Socrates, he lavished so much money on its decoration that people came to Pélla to see the palace, rather than the king.

The Peloponnesian War, with Athens and Sparta as rivals, began in 431 B.C. and exhausted most of the Greek city-states. There was general unrest as Athenian domination came to an end, and the indi-

Grey and white pebble mosaics still grace the floors in Pélla, capital of Alexander the Great.

vidual states themselves were rife with internal disputes. Meanwhile, neutral Macedonia grew in military strength.

The Rise of Macedonia

Rich in grain, gold and timber, Macedonia flared like a meteor under the political genius of Philip II. The Greek city-states, tired of endless fighting, hoped for unity. Athens tried in vain to withstand Philip's scheme of a federation of Greek states. The famous *Philippics* of Demosthenes, the Athenian orator, were aimed at maintaining this resistance.

In 338 B.C. Philip invaded Boeotia and defeated the united armies of Athens and Thebes in the Battle of Chaeronea. He subsequently assembled a convention in Corinth to declare the union of the Greeks and decide on war against Persia. But in 336 B.C., before he could set out on his Persian campaign, Philip was assassinated at Aegae during the wedding of his daughter Cleopatra. It took his son, Alexander, to fulfil his visionary aim of national unity and expansion.

Alexander the Great

Macedonia's finest hour occurred in the 4th century B.C. under the rulership of Alexander the Great. A brilliant, ambitious and ruthless young man, Alexander was only 18 when he commanded the left wing of the Macedonian army in the battle of Chaeronea. His tutor, Aristotle, a native Macedonian, had taught him to "live nobly". Now he succeeded to his father's empire and inherited his father's far-reaching ambitions.

Two years after Philip's death, Alexander crossed into Asia Minor and was victorious from the start. He advanced against Syria and Phoenicia, founded Alexandria on the Nile Delta and marched on to Bactria and Sogdiana in Upper Persia. His success carried him all the way to India. Recognition of his military genius did not satisfy Alexander, and he commanded the Greeks to recognize him as a god, the son of Zeus. Demosthenes, unreconciled, as bitter and sceptical about the son as he had been about the father, openly sneered. He committed suicide in 322 B.C.

Alexander contracted a fever and died in Babylon in 323 B.C. at the age of 33. He was responsible for spreading the Greek language and culture over three continents. But none of the Macedonian generals who survived him were strong **15** enough to hold the mighty empire together, and it was divided up into separate kingdoms.

Nonetheless, philosophy and the arts flourished. Epicurus and Zeno were the great thinkers of this period, and masterpieces like the *Venus of Milo* and the *Victory of Samothrace* were being produced. Ptolemy founded the famous library in Alexandria and turned the Egyptian city into a brilliant cultural magnet. Pergamum and Antioch were also important cultural centres.

Macedonia itself was weakened by wars and internal quarrels. The Roman state was expanding abroad. The defeat of the Macedonian King Perseus at Pydna in 168 B.C. brought to an end both a long succession of wars and the Macedonian empire. In 148 B.C. Macedonia became a Roman province, along with the rest of Greece.

Roman Rule

It was under the Romans that Salonica came into its own. The city had been founded by one of Alexander's generals. It was the most important commercial and military station on the Via Egnatia, the road built by the Romans during the second half of the 2nd century B.C. The nucleus of what was to become an important Jewish community was already established.

Greece was well treated under the Romans from the reign of Augustus on. Young Romans of noble birth were sent there to acquire education and culture. The Greek language had spread to the remotest parts of the known world, and educated Romans made a point of learning it. Roman families employed Greeks to teach their children. As the Latin poet Horace put it, "Captive Greece made captive her rude conqueror". The Greek tradition of abstract thought and the cosmopolitan Greek language were ripe to transmit a new ingredient to Western thought as the Christian church struggled to establish itself.

The chief figure of its early years was the Apostle Paul. He landed at the port of Neapolis (present-day Kavála) and continued to Philippi, where he baptized the woman Lydia. Afterwards he went to Salonica, where he preached in the synagogue. His first *Epistle to the Thessalonians*, written in Corinth only a few weeks after he left the city, is recognized as one of the oldest New Testament documents.

The Byzantine Empire

Raids into Greece by northern tribes began in the 2nd century A.D. The vast Roman empire had grown unwieldy and difficult to rule. Diocletian divided it into a western and an eastern half, ruling from the East rather than Rome. Subsequently, the two halves were further divided into a tetrarchy. The Emperor Constantine gave Christianity his official sanction. He reunited the East and West and established a new capital in the East at Byzantium, re-named Constantinople. Greek in culture and ideas, Constantinople became the Christian capital of the East-

Salonica's Arch of Galerius shows scenes of Roman triumphs.

ern, or Byzantine, empire, which came into being in A.D. 395.

Invasions into Greece continued, and the north suffered from the onslaught of Goths in the 3rd century, Huns in the 5th, followed by Slavs and Avars in the 6th and 7th centuries. Salonica, secure behind fortified walls, withstood their assaults and the town prospered as a wealthy centre of literature and the arts. Within the Byzantine empire it was second only to Constantinople. **17**

The north was next harrassed by Saracens, who took Salonica in 904. They were followed by Serbs and Bulgars. The region, and indeed the whole empire, was divided by theological disputes. Despite this, Byzantine culture reached its highest peak in the 10th century under the Macedonian dynasty. Splendid monasteries and churches were built on Mount Áthos and in Salonica. Their mosaics, manuscripts, book-bindings and miniatures attest to a glory that lingered for two centuries more.

After 1025, a series of weak rulers came to power and Byzantine territory in Italy was lost to Norman adventurers. Asia Minor was overrun by the Seljuk Turks. Theological differences continued to divide the Church and brought about a final schism between the Pope and the Patriarch in 1054 that has continued to this day.

The emergence of the Comneni dynasty allowed the empire to survive further raids by Normans and Turks. But the Byzantines fought to no avail against the soldiers of the Fourth Crusade, who occupied both Constantinople (1204) and Salonica (1202). The empire was partitioned into several small states, one of which was ruled by Michael VIII Paleologus. He succeeded in the reconquest of Constantinople in 1261 and founded the dynasty that would be last to rule the empire. While the Byzantine world was considerably reduced in size and importance, artistic life developed unabated.

Turkish Conquest

The Byzantine empire was on the decline when the Ottoman Turks set foot in Europe in 1354. They conquered one town after another. Salonica was handed over to the Venetians from 1423–30 in an attempt to save it, but the city's optimism turned to despair under the new rulers. In 1430 the Ottoman leader Murad II attacked the city, and after three days of siege, it finally fell to the Turks. Salonica lost its Byzantine glitter. It even lost its name and became Selanik. In 1453 Constantinople itself fell. Thásos was acquired in 1455 and Samothrace in 1457. By 1715 the entire Peloponnese was under Turkish rule.

Murad and his successors settled the most fertile areas of Macedonia and Thrace with **19**

Byzantine brickwork enhances many a church in Northern Greece.

Turks and forcibly relocated the Greeks, many of whom fled to Italy, the Ionian Islands and Georgia in the Caucasus. Turkish authorities were uneasy about the condition of depressed, semi-deserted Salonica and encouraged the emigration of thousands of Jews from Sicily, southern Italy, Portugal and Spain. The latter continued to speak Ladino, a form of mediaeval Spanish, into the 20th century and revived intellectual and commercial life.

By the middle of the 17th century, Salonica was alive again, a swarming, colourful city. There were hundreds of Turkish houses with enclosed courtyards filled with vines, flowers and splashing fountains. Almost everyone spoke Turkish or Hebrew. Salonica was beautiful, then, in a way distinctly oriental—but the Greeks were a subject people.

The Struggle for Independence

While the Byzantine empire fell, the Christian Church survived. Priests and monks kept alive a Greek nationalist spirit in places like Metéora and Mount Áthos. This grew stronger after 1715, when the Turkish conquest was complete, and was further stimulated by the French Revolution.

The general debt owed by the rest of Europe to ancient Greece served to make the cause of Greek independence from the Turks especially attractive, and sympathy for the Greeks was fanned by the poet Byron, among others. (Byron died at Missolonghi, where he had gone in aid of the struggling nation.) With Russia as well as England and France eventually joining up to support Greece during the War of Independence that broke out in 1821, victory was assured in 1832, and a new Greek monarchy was installed the following year.

However, Northern Greece remained under the Sultan's government. Unrest in Macedonia and Thrace grew into the "Macedonian Struggle". Greece took advantage of the situation and pressed claims for territory still under Turkish rule. The chances of ultimate success were increased by the fact that the once mighty Turkish empire was in a state of decline.

Eleftherios Venizelos, a Cretan politician several times prime minister of Greece, entered into negotiations for the liberation of Epirus, Macedonia and Thrace. But within Turkey, a group of vigorous nationalists known as the

Young Turks had taken power, and were determined not to cede any more of the Empire. Greek proposals were therefore rejected, and the First Balkan War followed in 1912. Within a few months, the Greek army entered Salonica. The city was free after almost 500 years, and parts of Epirus, Macedonia and Thrace were secured.

Greece won yet more territory after the Second Balkan War, but there was little time to enjoy freedom before involvement in World War I. At its conclusion, Greece acquired Eastern and Western Thrace; only to cede the former to Turkey, now under the leadership of Kemal Ataturk, by terms of the Treaty of Lausanne (1923). Many islands were lost to Greece as well.

Population-exchange agreements with Turkey in 1923

Guardians of Mount Áthos: monks return to their ancient republic.

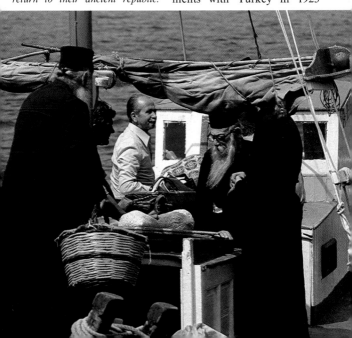

resulted in an influx into Greece of some 1½ million Greek refugees, about half of whom settled in the north. Vast public works projects were undertaken; road-building, irrigation, drainage and flood control opened up the hinterland, making it habitable and productive.

Modern Times

Greece was declared a republic in 1924, and though King George II was recalled in 1935, he acceded to the military dictatorship of Ioannis Metaxas months later. The dictator remained in power from 1936 until his death in January 1941. Metaxas is best remembered for his legendary reply to Mussolini's surrender ultimatum, given in October 1940—a short, resounding "no". Greece entered World War II voluntarily on the Allied side and defeated the Italians. Nazi Germany invaded Greece in April 1941 and by June controlled most of the country. Almost all Salonica's Jewish population (about 60,000) were deported to Poland, never to return.

After liberation in November 1944, crisis followed crisis, with communists and royal partisans at odds. Christmas Day of 1944 found both the

Prime Minister of Britain, Winston Churchill, and his Foreign Secretary, Anthony Eden, in Athens, so urgent was the need to establish a firm, anticommunist regime in Greece. War and enemy occupation had already devastated the country. Foreign trade, especially with Germany, a major pre-war customer for Northern Greece's tobacco crop, was at a standstill. The United States supplied economic aid to Greece (seen in the West as a vital bastion against the further spread of communist power) under the Truman Doctrine, but the internal political scene worsened, culminating in two

years of civil war and a communist defeat in 1949.

In 1967, continuing unrest gave rise to a military dictatorship. Young King Constantine flew north to rally support, but the army gave its allegiance to the colonels and he fled to Rome while the régime continued in power for seven years. The Greek economy was at rock bottom by the time this dictatorship crumbled and democracy was restored. On November 17, 1974, the first general elections for ten years were held in Greece. A few weeks later the people voted against restoration of the monarchy.

Modernity and Grecian beauty combine at a Salonica fun-fair.

For Macedonia and Thrace, union with Greece came late and was scarcely enjoyed before the region was involved in the conflicts of this century. Now, at last, Northern Greece can achieve its full potential as a thriving agricultural and commercial area. Visitors are responding to the promotion of tourism, with its promise of the new-old splendours of sun, beach and history. Ahead lies the prospect of collaboration with Europe as Greece defines its role in the Common Market. **23**

Where to Go

Northern Greece covers a big area and there's a lot to see, but many important sights are within reasonable distance of Salonica. The ancient towns of Pélla, Édessa, Lefkádia, Véria and Vergína can all be visited in one day. Kastoriá and Metéora are popular two-day excursions. Kavála, with convenient connections to Thásos, is not much more than 150 kilometres away.

Tours to these outlying points of interest leave from Salonica. For some you can be fetched from main Halkidiki hotels. There is also regular transport between Halkidiki and the city. Getting around is naturally easiest by car, but hired cars are very expensive.

It's Greek to Me

Finding your way around in Northern Greece will be much easier if you learn the Greek Alphabet. This isn't as difficult as it sounds. All street signs and some road indications are written in capital letters—many of which are already familiar to you. See ALPHABET on page 102 for a quick course in reading Greek.

In this book we have used time-honoured English spellings for well-known places like Salonica, Halkidiki and Samothrace, while indicating their modern Greek names in parentheses. Elsewhere we have given the transcriptions of the Greek names as the most useful means of asking your way.

The transcription system used in Greece itself is in a state of virtual chaos, and you'll find, for example,

Ágios, *Hágios* and *Ághios* (meaning Saint) indifferently.

Stress, a very important feature of the Greek language, is indicated by an accent mark (´) over the vowel of the syllable to be emphasized.

Two words you'll want to learn immediately are ΠΛΑΤΕΙΑ *(platía)*, meaning square, and ΟΔΟΣ *(odós)*, street, which are often omitted in addresses. Here are translations of some other Greek words to help you in reading the maps:

Agía	
Ágii	Saint(s), Holy
Ágios	
Ósios	
Kólpos	Gulf
Leofóros	Avenue
Límni	Lake
Óros	Mountain
Panagía	Our Lady
Profítis	Prophet
Tachidromío	Post Office

Salonica

(Thessaloníki)

Modern thoroughfares, fashionable boutiques, a streamlined waterfront and an international trade fair site—all this is only a façade for the Byzantine heart that still beats in Salonica. Cassander, one of Alexander's generals, founded the city in 316 B.C. (He had the political good sense to marry Alexander's half-sister and the domestic good sense to confer her name on the town.) Salonica grew in importance until it became second only to Constantinople during the Byzantine epoch. Most of the monuments of that golden age survive, though many suffered damage in devastating fires.

While there are reminders, too, of 500 years of Turkish rule, most of the old brick and wood buildings burned to the ground. There were four big fires in the 19th century and the streets used to resound with the cries of the *tulúmbasis,* or Jewish firemen, dragging primitive pumps. In 1917 fire wiped out the major part of Salonica, making way for today's city of more than 800,000 inhabitants.

Salonica rises like an amphitheatre from the Bay of Salonica to the spur of Mount Chortiátis. The city's long-standing commercial importance results from its favourable situation on the Thermaic Gulf. Not only does it have a natural outlet to the sea, but it is also logically placed for serving the needs of the hinterland.

The most practical way to visit the city is on one of the excellent guided tours. Most such tours originate at Halkidiki hotels, but some also begin in Salonica itself. Salonica, however, is a perfectly walkable city even if its extremely hot

summer temperatures are not conducive to exercise: best confine on-foot sightseeing to mornings and evenings.

You'll no doubt want to devote special attention to the Byzantine churches. Remember to take opera glasses or binoculars to view wall paintings and mosaics. The Folklore and Archaeological museums, if technically included in some set tours, are worth long, independent visits, to see the displays at leisure.

City Sights

The **White Tower** (*Lefkós Pírgos*), symbol of Salonica, dominates the waterfront, and the wide seaside promenade, Leofóros Níkis, leads directly to it. This landmark, greyish-white and stocky, stands alongside the harbour like an oversized chess piece.

The sunset-hour vólta *leads along the waterfront promenade to the White Tower, symbol of Salonica.*

The Vólta

When the sun goes down and evening breezes cool the air, Greeks young and old take a ritual stroll known as the *vólta*. Every town has an area set aside for the daily promenade. Salonica's is the waterside stretch between Platía Aristotélous and the White Tower—a gentle ten-minute saunter.

Women wear their crispest cottons and men their smartest shirts. Proud parents show off their children, young couples meet and older people exchange greetings. This pleasant social custom brings the whole town together.

This 15th-century tower formed part of Salonica's old sea wall, and its history is less than serene. One of its names, "Tower of Blood", referred to its use as a prison. In the final years of the 19th century, the Turkish Sultan ordered the tower white-washed, hoping to erase the unhappy memories it represented. Today the White Tower is a meeting place for sea scouts and looks down on the sunset-hour *vólta*.

It is appropriate that the White Tower now houses a **museum** dedicated to the history of Salonica, covering the early Christian to late Byzantine periods. Articles on display include city plans, sketches, Christian tombs, wall paintings and other archaeological finds. The whole crowned by a roof garden and refreshment bar.

East of the gardens, the International Trade Fair site covers a huge area of land. The fair in its present form was started in 1926 and is held annually in September. It is descended from the Demetria, an old merchant festival that honoured Demetrius, the patron saint of Salonica. Don't confuse this with the modern Demetria, a festival of cultural events held every October.

If you are doing without the comfort of a guided tour and stepping it out on your own, the walk from the fair site to the Odós Egnatía is relatively short. This street offers its share of Roman ruins: an arch, a palace and a hippodrome. There is also a rotunda near by.

The area around the **Arch of Galerius** *(Apsída Galeríou)*, known locally as the Kamára, must have been the most splendid part of the city during the Roman tetrarchy, when Galerius Maximian chose Salonica as his place of residence. The arch was built to commemorate the emperor's victories over the Persians in A.D. 297.

This young apprentice is the inheritor of a venerable tradition. The demanding art of icon painting has been practised since Byzantine times.

Originally there were four main pillars supporting a cupola, with smaller arches on each side. Today only one of the main piers with its supporting arch remains. The brick structure, faced with stone reliefs, is crowded with figures of men and horses. The sacrifice scene, on the second zone from the bottom, is the best preserved.

Galerius (in officer's uniform) and Diocletian are shown on either side of an altar, giving thanks for Galerius' military triumphs. On the southern side of the arch was the entrance to a large hall, visible today below ground level.

The Rotunda of Saint George *(Ágios Geórgios)* stands on a rise above the arch. The domed 4th-century structure was intended as a mausoleum for Galerius, but he died abroad and was unable to lie in his monument. A century later the building was converted into a Christian church, and several architectural changes were made to accommodate it to Christian worship.

The most important was the erection of a new wall around the original circular one. The eight recesses that open into it are covered with rich mosaic decoration. More mosaic work ornaments the dome. Although the central figure of Christ has disappeared, the heads of some of the encircling angels are still visible. The superb remaining **mosaics** show martyr saints, their arms outstretched in prayer.

The building, used as a mosque during Turkish occupation, is now a museum of early Christian art, unfortunately closed to the public as a result of earthquake damage in 1978. Restoration is planned, but there is no firm date for reopening.

Near at hand in the Odós Egnatía are small shops where you can watch the art of icon painting still going on and buy examples (see p. 85). Follow this street to the Platía Agía Sofías and the domed basilica of the same name. This is one of five historic churches situated in a group to the west of the Rotunda. Note that most of them close during the afternoon siesta from 1 to 5 p.m.

Like its counterpart in Constantinople, **Agía Sofía** was constructed in honour of the wisdom *(sofía)* of God. The church (currently under restoration) is thought to have been erected some time in the 8th century, judging from its transitional style (see box pp. 32–33). You'll notice that the dome—a new feature—rests somewhat awkwardly on squinches, or supports projecting from a square base, rather than on a circular one. Nevertheless, the over-all effect is impressive, due in large part to mosaics showing the Ascension of Christ, the Virgin and the Apostles. The Theodosian capitals come from an earlier church. They are decorated with the wind-blown acanthusleaf motif popular during the reign of Theodosius II, Emperor of Byzantium.

A few streets away is **Panagía Achiropiítos,** one of the earliest examples of Christian architecture in Salonica. It was built in honour of the Virgin after the Council of Ephesus recognized her as the Mother of God in A.D. 431. The church, a basilica, occupies the site of an old Roman villa. Of particular interest are the splendid Theodosian capitals.

The name of the church means "Not Made by Human Hands". This refers to a miraculous icon it housed, said to have been fashioned by divine intervention, rather than human skill. With the fall of Salonica to the Turks, Panagía

The church of Panagía Chalkéon has always been associated with the coppersmith's art, even under the Turks, who converted it to a mosque.

Byzantine Church Architecture

Salonica's churches run the gamut of the Byzantine style and illustrate its evolution from the primitive basilica and domed central hall into the complex Greek-cross plan that best symbolizes the spirituality of the Orthodox Church.

The first Christian congregations modelled their places of worship on the Roman basilica or meeting hall, with its flat wooden ceiling or barrel vault (Ágios Dimítrios, 5th century). They also adapted the domed central church hall for use as baptisteries or memorials to martyrs (Ágios Geórgios, 4th century).

An engineering breakthrough in the 6th century made it possible to combine the rectangular floor plan of the basilica with the domed roof of the central church hall. The result can be seen in Ágia Sofía, a domed basilica built early in the 8th century.

But Byzantine architectural developments were influenced by spir-

Basilica

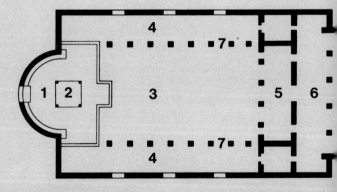

1. *apse (semi-circular termination)*   2. *altar*   3. *nave*   4. *aisles*
5. *narthex (vestibule)*   6. *exonarthex (vestibule preceding or following*
32 *façade)*   7. *columns*

itual considerations as well as technical advances. In the 7th century, the Christian symbol of the cross—the Greek cross with arms of equal length—was added to the floor plan (Panagía Chalkéon, 11th century; Ágii Apóstoli, 14th century). However, you may find it difficult to perceive the cruciform design, due to the proliferation of side chapels and annexes.

For Orthodox congregations, the dome and vault overhead signifies heaven. Thus the most important figures in the rich decorative scheme of frescoes or mosaics occupy the highest places: Christ in the dome, Mary in the semi-vault of the apse, the Evangelists in the transitional zone below. Along the walls, the great Biblical stories were depicted for those who couldn't read. The lowest level was reserved for the saints and fathers of the Church.

The interior was designed to direct the attention of worshippers towards the sanctuary, then up the walls to the opening of the dome, giving visible form to a mystic and spiritual encounter with God.

Greek-cross Church

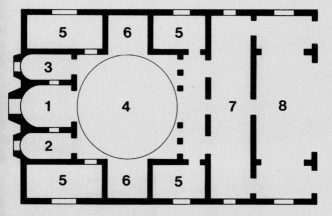

1. *bema (sanctuary)* 2. *prothesis (room for preparation and storage of Eucharist)* 3. *diaconicon (archive, library, vestry)* 4. *dome* 5. *chapels* 6. *transverse bar of the cross* 7. *narthex* 8. *exonarthex*

Achiropíitos became a mosque. Its popular name, Agía Paraskeví, is derived from the Greek word for "Friday", the Moslem day of worship.

The small brick church of **Panagía Chalkéon** is situated near by in a corner of the Platía Dikastiríon, just off Odós Egnatía. It was commissioned

by Christophoros, an imperial dignitary, for the redemption of his sins and those of his wife. The church was one of the first in Salonica to be constructed in the cruciform style. Restora- tions this century have respected its original features, and some old frescoes survive in a damaged state.

Immediately after 1430, when the church was converted

Fine mosaics decorate many of Salonica's churches. Some exteriors (like Ágios Dimítrios, right) have undergone reconstruction over the centuries.

Saint Demetrius

The people of Salonica believed Demetrius guarded the city from danger. The saint could raise tempests that put enemy fleets to flight and topple would-be invaders from the ramparts. A dazzling figure in a streaming white cloak, Demetrius resolutely turned back the city's enemies.

He was known as the "Champion" and the "City's Friend". Believers spoke of his healing powers. Divine perfumes were said to be given off by a relic kept near his tomb. Weighty indeed was an oath sworn in the name of Saint Demetrius.

Oddly enough, the Greek army liberated Salonica on the eve of the Saint's festival in 1912. On October 26, the day of the festival itself, the Turks signed the protocol of surrender. As a result, Saint Demetrius' Day gained even greater significance.

which explains why most of the shops display a hefty-looking pair of scales in a prominent position.

In the area is one of the main commercial streets of the city, Odós Eleftheríou Venizélou.

The largest flower in this Byzantine bouquet is **Ágios Dimítrios,** a church dedicated to Saint Demetrius, a Christian noble martyred at the command of Galerius. The present structure is a faithful reproduction of the 5th-century basilica destroyed in the great 1917 fire. In the crypt you can see remains of the original shrine built over the tomb of the martyr, as well as the ruins of the Roman baths where Demetrius was confined and killed.

In the course of restoration, many old marble columns of unequal height were taken from other buildings and installed here. As in early Christian times, they have been erected on pedestals of different heights. The capitals include some with Theodosian acanthus leaves; others sport eagles with outspread wings.

Many **mosaics** were lost in the 1917 fire. Those remaining are particularly fine: one shows Demetrius with Leontius, who commissioned the 5th-century building after he was miracu-

into a mosque, it was called the "Mosque of the Smiths". The modern Greek name, literally "Our Lady of the Coppersmiths", is simply a translation of this. The street which gives it its name still runs alongside, a blaze of shining metal pots, pans and ornaments. Some of the items are sold by weight,

lously healed by the saint. In another, Demetrius appears with church officials responsible for repairing the church after a fire in the 7th century. Here, as elsewhere, the saint's face is youthful and idealized.

Take a taxi to Ágii Apóstoli, which stands right alongside remains of the old city wall.

The market displays sausages, cheese, olives in abundance for the creation of regional delicacies.

Taxis are cheap and plentiful in Salonica, so it is not an expensive business to avoid too much exertion in sightseeing.

The 14th-century exterior of **Ágii Apóstoli** boasts the richest brick decoration of mediaeval Salonica. The complex patterns display all the intricacy of mosaic work. This cruciform church is the least-restored of Salonica's religious monuments. Inside are splendid examples of the last flowering of Byzantine art during Paleolo-

gan times. One charming mosaic portrays the bathing of the infant Jesus. A solicitous midwife is shown testing the heat of the water, while the baby twists apprehensively in his nurse-maid's arms.

Much depends now on whether you wish to see more Byzantine architecture: Ósios David, Agía Ekateríni, Ágios Nikólaos Orfanós, Profítis Ilías. If all this ornamental brickwork is beginning to look like packet after packet of ginger biscuits pressed down and shaken together, stop for a good, long, iced coffee. Then, as a contrast to the calm sanctity of Byzantium, you can always dodge off for an hour in the market.

The **Bezesténi** is situated at the rear of a disused Turkish bath house (damaged by the 1978 earthquake and under repair) near Odós Venizélou and Odós Egnatía, across the road from Panagía Chalkéon. Mingle with the local people who shop here for clothes and household necessities. There are watch repair shops and jewellers in the area, too. Even if you don't carry away a bargain, you'll be surrounded by the bazaar atmosphere that once gave Salonica all the colour and magic of an oriental city.

There is more noise, confusion and chatter at the nearby food market in a group of covered arcades called the **Stoá Modiáno.** Butchers, fishmongers and greengrocers all vie for attention. You can buy almost anything, from hearty tomatoes to sugary sweetmeats. So shop at the Bezesténi for a basket to carry it all home.

Picturesque houses and small, tangled gardens dot Salonica's **acropolis,** situated towards the north near the Turkish quarter. You can inspect the remains of the old ramparts (*kástra*) that once enclosed the city and look out over Salonica to the bay. The castle at the top is called the Eptapírgia (no visits).

Outskirts of Salonica

At the resort suburb of **Panórama,** 10 kilometres south-east of Salonica in the Mount Chortiátis foothills, views of the surrounding countryside are as spectacular as the name suggests. Bracing air, good *tavérnes* and a selection of hotels, night clubs and discotheques are added attractions. Be sure to sample a local pastry speciality called *trígonas*, delicious custard-filled horns covered with honey.

Museums

Greek museums are oases of cool, airy enjoyment, and Salonica's are no exception to this happy rule. Note that all museums in the city close on Tuesday and admit visitors free of charge on Sunday.

The **Archaeological Museum** *(Archeologikó Mousío)* is a stone's throw from the White Tower. On show are finds from all over Northern Greece, including pottery, weapons, jewellery and carvings from Neolithic to Byzantine times. Pride of place is given to objects from Macedonian tombs, especially the royal tomb of Philip II, still under excavation at Vergína (see p. 73).

(see p. 73)

You cannot fail to be impressed by this Macedonian treasure-trove. There are sumptuous wreaths of gold laurel and oak leaves and exquisitely wrought jewellery. Two superb *larnaxes* or funerary chests are made of solid gold, the larger of the two weighing some 22 pounds. Both are decorated on the lid with a majestic 16-ray star, symbol of the Macedonian monarchy.

Ongoing excavations continue to enrich museum holdings. A fabulous hoard of gold objects from ancient Síndos, unearthed in 1980, is on dis-

This ivory head of Philip II is among the Macedonian treasures unearthed in Vergina excavations.

play, including haunting burial masks and elaborate filigree jewellery.

The pretty little **Ethnological and Folklore Museum** *(Mousío Laikís Téchnis)* is situated in the southern part of the city. It occupies a delightful old house at 68 Vasilíssis Ólgas, typical of Salonican villas before the era of plate-glass and concrete. Fine examples of Greek national costume are on display, as well as household items, weapons and some exquisite embroidery.

Halkidiki
(Chalkidikí)

Twenty years ago most people had never heard of Halkidiki. Now, not only have they heard of it, many of them can even pronounce it. You huff hard on the "h" and place the stress fair and square on the last syllable: hal-kee-dee-KEE. It sounds almost like a wave breaking. The area lies to the south and east of Salonica. It juts from the northern mainland like Poseidon's trident, say the romantics. The bays of Kassándra and Singitikós penetrate deeply into it, dividing the southern part into three long headlands—Kassándra, Sithonía and Ágion Óros (Áthos).

The whole region covers over 1,000 square miles. Mountains run north-west to southeast. The fertile plains are an immense grain-bowl, silvered by a scattering of olive trees. Beautiful beaches rim much of the coastline, and the climate is hot and dry in summer. Halkidiki really is a big, natural holiday paradise, marked, like the mainland itself, by geographical contrast.

The main town and regional capital is POLÍGIROS, with a population of no more than 6,000. While a small museum here shows finds from all over Halkidiki, major discoveries are to be seen at the Archaeological Museum in Salonica. It is, however, worth making an effort to visit **Petrálona Cave** *(Kókkines Pétres)*, directly west of Políros. (Explorations continue, so opening times are uncertain. The best way of seeing them is through your hotel, tour group or a local tour agency.) The unassuming landscape surrounding the cave gives no indication of the awesome magnificence of a network of beige and rose caverns underground. There are steel pathways to walk on. Displays of primitive human habitation and animal remains are housed in the museum nearby.

Tour agencies offer day trips to places of interest in the area, fetching tourists in Salonica or from the main Halkidiki hotels. One such excursion takes you east to **Arnéa,** a hill town devoted to the spinning and weaving of wool. Women are the main producers of woven carpets, tapestries and long-pile *flokáti* rugs in what is almost entirely a cottage industry. The

Picturesque Arnéa in the hills is the home of the famed spinners and weavers of rural Halkidiki.

HALKIDIKI

balconies of the houses are strung with natural wool set out to dry. There is plenty of opportunity to buy an example of local handiwork straight from the loom or from one of the small shops that surround the town square.

Aristotle's birthplace, STÁGIRA, is not far away. It is notable only for a large, rather depressing statue of the great man, who stares with unphilosophic grimness at a distant telegraph pole. You continue east through rolling hills to STRATÓNI, on the east coast of Halkidiki, then to IERISSÓS, a boat-building and fishing village.

From there, going south, it is only 7 kilometres to NÉA RÓDA, a town near the minor depression which was once Xerxes' canal. The isthmus is estimated to have risen considerably since the canal was dug by the Persians in 480 B.C. to facilitate invasion and avoid a risky boat trip around the tip of Mount Áthos. Now it is only a slight scar on the landscape. In this region there are some splendid beaches.

Some 8 kilometres more bring you to **Ouranoúpolis**, literally "Heavenly Town". It lies on the frontier of Mount Áthos and was founded by refugees from Turkey in 1922. The wa-terfront tower was built in the 12th century by the Emperor Andronicus II as a look-out against pirates. Now it is a take-off and landing place for hundreds of swallows playing endless games of swoop and dive. The western sky glows with the orange, saffron and jade of the sunsets, and white-washed houses are sweet and clean under their leafy porches. Some of the inhabitants make attractive rugs, an industry revived by an Australian woman who spent much of her life in the town.

But the beaches are the real attraction of the area, rapidly bringing Halkidiki to the forefront of the international tourist industry. They can be reached by a frequent, regular bus service from Salonica.

Among them is **Thermaikoú Beach** at AGÍA TRIÁDA, 29 kilometres from Salonica. Here the vacation facilities of hotel and camping ground are set right alongside a waterfront village. It is a convivial combination, since a stroll along the sand opens up the possibility of *tavérnes*, shopping and getting to know the local people. This is not always the case at the major tourist installations, where the nearest township is sometimes some distance away.

Eighty kilometres from Salonica is the large, bungalow-studded complex that fronts the beach at **Gerakíni,** situated between the first two peninsulas. Gerakína, so the story goes, was a girl who used to meet her lover nightly by a well. When he tired of her she drowned herself there. Now the well and the area around it carry her name. The setting is one of smooth lawns, flower gardens and ancient olive groves.

⸙ Kassándra

The gentle contours of the 150-mile Kassándra coastline (named after Alexander the Great's general Cassander) make for long, sweeping beaches. It is no wonder that most large-scale tourist developments are concentrated here. A wide range of facilities is offered at such holiday centres as SÁNI, KALITHÉA, KRIOPIGÍ, CHANIÓTI and PALIOÚRI. This includes protected swimming areas and swimming pools, bars, restaurants, discotheques, boutiques, tennis and volley-ball courts. You can hire sports equipment, and at some resorts there is mini-golf and horse-riding. For a small fee, non-resident visitors can join in.

Government-run camping grounds are impeccably clean and efficient. Huge trees, creepers and hedges lend privacy to individual grassy sites. The National Tourist Organization of Greece is justifiably proud of them. There are numbers of small hotels, too, as well as rooms to let in private houses.

A good road circles the whole peninsula. You can turn off the main road to picturesque fishing villages, where brightly coloured boats rock at anchor. Fresh fish and fruit are plentiful at beach-side restaurants. But if you're driving, beware of the early afternoon and late evening traffic. People from Salonica can't get to Kassándra fast enough.

A few of the towns on Kassándra have a historic past, but not much to offer in the way of archaeological sights. Some of them were settled by Greek immigrants from Asia Minor, who arrived during the tremendous population exchange of the 1920s. Their villages were named after places they had left, with the addition of the prefix *néos* or *néa* meaning "new". These immigrants brought life and activity back to an area deserted since the Turkish Pasha of Salonica ordered the inhabitants killed and their houses razed during the struggle for independence.

Sithonía

Sparsely populated Sithonía offers some of the loveliest scenery in Northern Greece. A new road travels along some 180 miles of breathtaking coastline, where tiny beaches afford absolute privacy and perfect calm. Inland, the forests of Mount Lóngos are dark and cool with streams and springs. You can breathe the scent of

The Sithonía promontory offers pine-ringed coves and sweeping sandy beaches, unspoiled fishing villages and the modernity of Pórto Carrás.

pine in an almost alpine stillness. All this, plus the strong Halkidiki sun, makes Sithonia the most appealing of the three contrasting fingers of land.

There are attractive villages and camping spots. TORÓNI is a fine beach and PÓRTO KOUFÓ in the south an excellent natural harbour. There are splendid views of Mount Áthos from around KALAMÍTSI, and the delightful fishing hamlet of ÓRMOS PANAGÍAS on the north-east coast looks out on the DIÁPOROS, a scattering of islets sprinkled over the sparkling waters of the gulf.

While accommodation on Sithonía is in general modest, sophistication is to be found at **Pórto Carrás** near NÉOS MARMARÁS. The holiday complex comprises two hotels and a village inn, two theatres, an 18-hole golf course, an excellent beach and a fine marina capable of accommodating luxury craft. This is *le grand chic* of Halkidiki, an idea born in the mind of Greek shipping magnate, John Carras.

The complex is backed by a large estate run as a model farm. It produces fruit, olives, almonds and fine wine grown from French cuttings under the supervision of experts from the Bordeaux region of France.

Mount Áthos
(Ágion Óros)

"Awesome", "dreadful" and "sacred" are epithets frequently applied to Halkidiki's eastern peninsula, a male preserve entirely devoted to the Orthodox religion. No female creature is permitted to set foot in the Theocratic Republic of Áthos, a self-administering member of the Greek State. Foreign visitors (men only, of course) require a letter of introduction from their consulates to the Greek Ministry of Foreign Affairs or the Ministry of Northern Greece (see SIGHTSEEING TOURS, p. 120).

Áthos has relented only slightly on the 11th-century ruling forbidding access to smooth-faced persons, female animals, children and eunuchs. While the monks themselves wear beards and long hair (as well as the *zostikón*, or black gown with leather girdle), clean-shaven male visitors are not likely to be turned away. Stays may not exceed three days and the number of independent visitors entering each day is limited.

A regular bus service operates from Salonica to Ouranoúpolis (144 km.) and from here caiques leave for DÁFNI, main port of the Áthos peninsula, named for its laurels.

The obligatory first stop for presentation of entry documents is **Kariés,** capital of the monastic community. You travel there by bus along the only paved road on the peninsula, built for the 1963 millenary celebrations. There is a post office and telephone facilities, as well as a small inn. Be sure to visit the **Protáton,** the Cathedral Church of Áthos, owned jointly by all the monasteries. It is a restored, 10th-cen-

The monks of Mount Áthos spend a life of contemplation and prayer among a heritage of mediaeval art.

tury basilica, noted for its frescoes painted by artists of the Macedonian school (see below).

From Kariés, travel is mostly on foot. Mules can be hired for the journey from one monastery to another, but it is customary to descend and approach the monastery gates (closed at sunset) on foot, a gesture of humility. Since food and accommodation are offered without charge, contributions should be made to monastic funds in keeping with the hospitality given. The pleasant local wine is served to guests, along with bread and olives, perhaps even fruit, though seldom more than this. Residents eat very little, often only one meal a day, and few ever partake of meat. It is a reasonable precaution to bring a supply of food and insect repellent. Photography is allowed, but cine-cameras and tape-recorders are strictly forbidden.

An immovable faith has sustained religious activity and Greek culture on Áthos for more than 1,000 years. The first monastery, the Megísti Lávra, was founded in the 10th century by Athanasius the Athonite. (Legend claims that either Saint Helena or the Virgin herself had a hand in it, thus explaining the subsequent refusal of other less eminent female visitors.) Afterwards, religious buildings multiplied. They once housed a community of some 20,000 monks, though not more than 1,500 are in residence today.

Of the 20 large monasteries, 17 are Greek and the other three Russian, Bulgarian and Serbian. They are divided into two categories, *coenobite*, where monks pool their resources, and *idiorrhythmic*, where there is more independence and the rules are less rigid. All monasteries but one follow the Julian calendar, 13 days behind the rest of Europe. Eight hours of every day are devoted to prayer, and another eight are spent at work. Study, penitence and sleep account for the rest of the monks' time. In addition there are sanctuaries, cottages and hermitages, some of them extremely isolated, where monks live singly or in small groups. A few work at agriculture or handicrafts; others fast, keep vigils and study the scriptures.

The monasteries have been pillaged of many of their treasures. Some consecrated objects were destroyed by fire and others sold in the early 1800s to raise funds for the cause of Greek independence. Nevertheless, Áthos remains a magnificent storehouse of precious relics, chalices, miniatures, mosaics and icons. There are books and illuminated manuscripts of prime importance, too. The monks are careful to preserve this heritage. They even add to it, in the form of art works reproduced in the tradition of the two great schools of Byzantine painting, the Macedonian and the Cretan.

These schools evolved during the 14th century in Northern Greece and on the island of Crete. The Macedonian painters adopted the sturdy realism of the masterful Manuel Panselinos. The Cretans modelled their work (characterized by dark backgrounds) after Theophanes' static, introverted conservatism. Fine examples of both schools of painting exist in the Mount Áthos monasteries.

Vatopédi, $2\frac{1}{2}$ hours by track from Kariés, is a good place to begin a tour of the monasteries. It is the most "modern" of them, thanks to rebuilding after a 1965 fire. The community's 11th-century church is decorated inside with frescoes of the Macedonian school. Porphyry columns support the central dome, a feature of the Greek-cross plan. The splendid bronze doors, dating from the 14th century, were brought here from Agía Sofía in Salonica. Also worthy of mention is the library, with its rare parchments, manuscripts and thousands of volumes.

Chiliandári, the Serbian monastery to the north-west, was established in the 12th century. Frescoes of the Macedonian school cover the walls of its church, and icons of the Cretan school are housed in the library. Noteworthy among the hundreds of manuscripts are rare Slavonic parchments.

The land journey to **Ivíron,** farther south, takes about 4 hours, but caiques from Vatopédi occasionally travel here. Monks from Georgia in the Caucasus founded the community in the 10th century and Russians contributed to its wealth. One notable donor was Peter the Great. His gift, an enormous Bible, is housed in the library along with other priceless volumes. A collection of valuable vestments is contained in the treasury.

A track runs through fertile country to **Megísti Lávra,** still farther south. This is the largest of the monasteries and the only one that has never suffered from fire. Cone-shaped Mount Áthos, named after a legendary giant of **49**

Simóno Pétra, one of the bastions of Christianity on Áthos, seems to have been chiselled from the rock of that holy mountain.

pre-Christian tradition, rises directly above the monastery and its dozens of churches.

The most important of them contains the grave of the 10th-century founder, Athanasius the Athonite, whose memorial service is magnificently celebrated on July 5. Another displays the 9-pound iron cross worn by the Saint during long divine services. Fine frescoes by Theophanes, who died at Megísti Lávra,

adorn monastery walls, and the library is rich in volumes and manuscripts.

On the return journey from Megísti Lávra to Dáfni, you pass by other monasteries and many inaccessible hermits' dwellings. Only in special cases are prolonged stays and visits to further monasteries permitted. Women and others can view the historic monuments of Áthos from the sea, ferried by launch along the western coast. Tours set sail from ÓRMOS PANAGÍAS on Sithonía and stop for lunch on the island of AMOULIANÍ.

Clearly visible from a launch are the monasteries of

East to the Border

Guided tours make the agreeable and interesting journey to Kavála (some 150 km. from Salonica) in one day. But you will almost certainly want to stay on and visit one of the most beautiful places in Northern Greece—the island of Thásos, just a few miles offshore. If so, travel to Kavála by coach, car or plane (the airport is situated at Chrisoúpolis, some 30 kilometres to the east of Kavála).

The run from Kavála to Alexandroúpolis (175 km.) is interesting if you have as your goal the island of Samothrace, with its fascinating history and archaeological remains. You can travel by coach from Kavála; by rail from Salonica. Note that the railway line east bypasses Kavála.

the **Dionisíou,** on a bleak rock above the sea, and the **Grigoríou,** erected on a rough headland in the 13th century and rebuilt after a fire in the 18th century. Winter storms cause the entire structure to shake. **Ágios Panteleímon,** the Russian monastery, stands out for its towers and gilded domes. The singing of its choirs used to be famous.

Real understanding of Áthos can, of course, only be gained by time spent within the monasteries. Visitors with an honest religious or studious interest will find a courteous welcome and simple hospitality.

Towards Kavála

From Salonica, the highway to Kavála heads north, then east, skirting the Lagadá and' Vólvi lakes. Between them, the small hamlet of LAGADÍKIA, make a short detour into the rural countryside. Turn left onto the asphalt road to SCHOLÁRI. After a short while, you arrive at a river. Ahead is a ford, but don't let your sense of adventure get the better of you. **51**

Turn left again, this time onto a perfectly acceptable dirt track, follow it for 200 yards, and, on your right, you'll see an enormous, dream-like plane tree with drooping branches and dark-green leaves.

This city of foliage is inhabited by hundreds of **herons.** a species protected by the government. If you leave the car and approach, they rise into the air by scores, flapping, circling and returning. Binoculars will help you watch the birds. A short distance along the same road, a similar tree with another protected colony rises from the flat landscape of reddish dust. Note that the herons may be seen during nesting, in April–June.

If you continue along the track, you come to an asphalt road that leads through tobacco- and fruit-growing country to LAGADÁS spa. This is where fire-walkers dance barefoot on hot embers during an interesting spring festival (see p. 91).

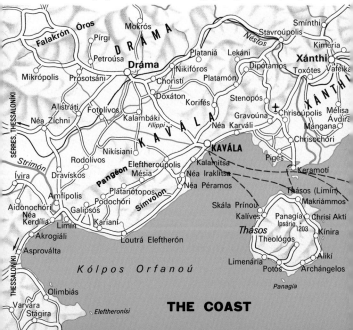

THE COAST

Back on the main road, you pass by LOUTRÁ VÓLVIS and the hot springs of NÉA APOLONÍA, considered good for rheumatic complaints. At ASPROVÁLTA the road finds the coast. You have, in fact, cut across the top of Halkidikí to the Gulf of Orfanoú. The fine beach here has been developed as a campsite by the National Tourist Organization of Greece.

Just after NÉA KERDÍLIA, the famed **Lion of Amfípolis** monument guards the approach to the River Strimón. This big fellow, very fine and fierce with well-curled mane and firmly planted forefeet, was fished out of the river-bed in pieces. The 4th-century B.C. statue was probably washed down from nearby AMFÍPOLIS, an important town in Alexander's day.

MOUNT PANGÉON dominates the Amfípolis landscape, a bushy scrub abounding in small game. The mountain was celebrated in ancient times as

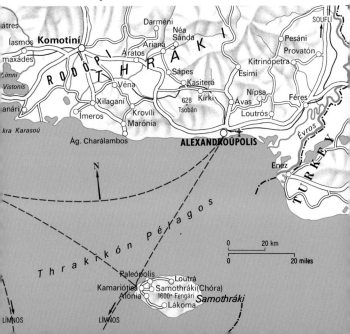

the site of an oracle of Diony-sus. Its rich gold and silver mines provoked a good deal of snapping and snarling between neighbouring states until Philip II put his foot down and claimed them for Macedonia.

From Amfípolis take the scenic road that follows the coast. There is one lovely beach after another along the final stretch to Kavála—from NÉA PÉRAMOS to KALAMÍTSA. It's up to you whether to try them all, but a good choice is at BÁTIS. The campsite is said to be the best in Northern Greece, high praise indeed, and a bus service connects the town to Kavála, 4 kilometres away.

The Man of Macedonia

Saint Paul was born a Jew and a free Roman citizen in Tarsus, a city in Asia Minor. His childhood language must have been Greek. He wrote all his Epistles in that lan-guage and quoted from the Greek version of the Old Tes-tament, known as the Septua-gint.

At some time he moved from Tarsus to Jerusalem, and it was there he encoun-tered the young Christian religion. At first, as an in-tensely religious and pious Pharisee, he persecuted the new Christians, but later he was converted by a vision of Christ on the road to Damas-cus. He changed his name from Saul to Paul, ceased his persecutions and became one of the most important figures in the early history of the Church.

Another revelation brought him to Macedonia and helped spread the Christian religion throughout Greece. Paul, with his two companions, Silas and Timothy, was in Troy when a vision appeared to him in the night: "There stood a man of Macedonia, and prayed him, saying, Come over into Macedonia and help us" *(Acts 16:9)*. The three men immediately made preparations for the voyage and "...came with a straight course to Samothracia and the next day to Neapolis; and from thence to Philippi, which is the chief city of that part of Macedonia and a colony..." *(Acts 16:11, 12)*.

Saint Paul's landing at Neapolis (present-day Kavá-la) was the end of a relatively simple journey from one Roman city to another. But it also marks Christianity's pas-sage from Asia to Europe.

The riches of sea and land meet at Kavála, an important fishing port and tobacco export harbour.

Kavála

Colourful Kavála, Macedonia's second largest city (population 65,000), rises in tiers from the waterfront up the slopes of Mount Símvolon. People here have a happy way with paint. Buildings sparkle, boats are gay combinations of red, yellow and blue—even the sky seems to have just been given a fresh coat. The harbour is busy with fishermen coiling ropes and piling nets, and seafood here is as good as anywhere on the Aegean.

This is a prosperous city, the centre of the Greek tobacco industry and the main point of export for the paddle-shaped

This fine aqueduct, built in the time of Suleiman the Magnificent, used to convey water to the hilltop citadel overlooking Kavála.

leaves. The local economy is also likely to benefit from the recent discovery of oil offshore, near Thásos.

In Saint Paul's time Kavála was known as Neapolis. It was the port for nearby Philippi and the usual landing for travellers from the Levant. Later it was called Christoupolis in honour of the founder of Saint Paul's religion, for the Apostle began his European mission here. The town was burned by the Normans, controlled by the Venetians and occupied by the Turks. Not until after World War I was it incorporated into Greece, along with the rest of Western Thrace.

A huge Turkish **aqueduct** *(kamáres)* dominates Kavála. Designed in the 16th century along Roman lines, the aqueduct carried water to the citadel, situated east on a promontory in the middle of the old town. It is pleasant to walk from the modern city centre to this picturesque old quarter.

Go up to the **acropolis** and stroll around the Byzantine walls for superb views. Then head down past the Imaret, a 19th-century group of courtyards, terraces and domes (unfortunately closed to the public) that served as an almshouse. Inmates enjoyed free food and exemption from military service, which caused the place to be known as the "Lazy Man's Home". The enterprise was financed by Mohammed Ali, founder of the modern Egyptian dynasty that ended with King Farouk.

Close by is Mohammed Ali's **house.** The monarch, son of a rich Albanian tobacco merchant, was born here in 1769. To be shown around, ring for the caretaker (avoiding siesta hours). You will see how the women of the house lived, locked away in their own quarters. They looked out at the world from behind latticed shutters and never appeared at male gatherings. There is an attractive garden at the back of the house and a swashbuckling equestrian statue of Mohammed Ali in the small square in front.

Also of interest is Kavála's worthy **Archaeological Museum** *(Archeologikó Mousío),* on the waterfront in the newer part of town. Finds from the city and nearby Amfípolis, Dráma and Sérres include carved stone tombs, coins, figurines and pottery.

Philippi
(Fílippi)

Buses bound for Dráma stop at the archaeological site of Philippi, just 15 kilometres north-west of Kavála. Philip II gave the town his name after he conquered it in 358 B.C., but historical associations are mainly Roman and early Christian.

It was here that Caesar's assassins, Brutus and Cassius, were defeated by Octavius and Antony in the famous battle that ended the Roman Republic in 42 B.C. The victors elevated the town to a Roman **57** colony where the Latin language was spoken and Roman law enforced. Little is known about its Macedonian population then. Jewish inhabitants must have been few, since there was no synagogue, only a place of worship near the river.

The excavations lie on either side of the modern road. On the north side, in an elevated area near the Byzantine walls, is the **theatre,** dating back to the 4th century B.C., but twice altered. The Romans staged gladiatorial contests here, but nowadays classical tragedies are again performed.

Also on this side of the road are the ruins of a sanctuary dedicated to Egyptian deities and fragmented remains of a

The ruins of Philippi contain memories of the historic battle that ended the Roman Republic and of the Apostle Paul, who preached the gospel here.

5th-century church called Basilica A. Just north of it is the **prison** where the Apostle Paul and his companion Silas were cast by the magistrates of the town. The story is recounted in *Acts 16*. As Paul and Silas prayed and sang, an earthquake suddenly wrenched the cell doors open and released the prisoners. The jailer wanted to stab himself, but Paul converted and baptized him instead. The next day Paul was implored to leave town, but he refused until his Roman citizenship was acknowledged and the magistrates had apologized in a terrified personal appearance.

Across the road is the **forum,** its outline still quite clear, and **Basilica B,** sometimes referred to as the *Direkler* (Turkish for "pillars"). The unfinished church collapsed under the weight of its dome and construction was abandoned. Adjoining it is an ancient and highly impressive public lavatory with some of the dignified marble seats still in place.

You may wish to continue on a short distance down the modern road to the river where Lydia, the first Macedonian convert to Christianity, was baptized. You turn left and walk over a bridge to a place of rushing water and shady trees. Local women come here to splash themselves and their children with droplets from the stream. A small church has been built nearby.

From Philippi the road runs over a plain golden with tobacco to DRÁMA, which does not live up to its name.

Thásos

The green circle of Thásos, the most northerly of Aegean islands, is set in a silver filigree of olive trees and sandy beaches. Local people are relaxed and welcoming, and the little island never seems overcrowded, even in the height of the tourist season. But then there are far fewer residents today than there were in ancient times—about 14,000 now against some 40,000 then.

Frequent ferries link Kavála and nearby KERAMOTÍ with the Thasian ports of Skála Prínou and Limín. Although a bus service operates on the island, it is worth taking a car. The roads are good. You can choose a hotel from the list conveniently posted on a notice board at the Limín quayside. There are facilities for campers, too.

A distinguished history and rich archaeological remains explain the special place Thásos holds in Greek affections. Famous in the 5th and the 4th **59** centuries B.C. for its snowy marble and fine wines, Thásos was also rich in gold, oil and timber. Amphorae (wine jars) bearing Thasian marks are still found in numbers off the coast, and some have turned up as far away as Sicily and Egypt.

Hippocrates, the founder of medical science, treated an epidemic of mumps here. The great painter Polygnotos was born on Thásos and so was the athlete Theogenes. It is said that this mighty man, who won 1,400 athletic prizes, once ate a whole bull for a wager. Gossip had it that his real father was the god Heracles, no weakling himself.

Old ways meet new: modern luxury resorts and rustic simplicity await fortunate visitors to Thásos, the most northerly island in the Aegean.

The modern port town of Thásos or **Limín** (short for Liménas) is built among ruins of the ancient city, and a wall of the 5th century B.C. still encloses a good part of it. The towers and gates are also preserved, although reconstructed in several places.

The wall rises steeply from the harbour to the **theatre.** This lovely creation of the 4th century B.C. has perfect acoustics. It is shaded by pines, and trees spring between the stone seats.

The proscenium, or stage, was dedicated to Dionysus long ago, and on summer evenings Greek classical drama is performed (see p. 90). The natural backdrop of the blue Aegean is so exquisite no set designer could contrive a better.

Further up is a simple, rock-hewn shrine to Pan with a relief of the god piping to his goats, shepherd's crook in hand.

The **Archaeological Museum** (*Archeologikó Mousío*), just off

Dionysus *(Bacchus)*

Dionysus was a god who provoked passion and ecstasy, whose cult was concerned with the creative powers of nature and man. Legend has it that he was the son of Zeus and Semele. Zeus (never short of amorous innovations) appeared to Semele in the form of a lightning flash, which destroyed her, but did not harm their child. The unborn child luckily was caught up and stitched into his father's thigh. Later the baby was carried to Mount Nysa, where satyrs aided nymphs and maenads in rearing the god. As he grew to manhood, the ritualistic merrymaking around him developed.

Although normally thought of as the god of wine, his religion was far more subtle and far-reaching than mere drunken revelry. Certain seasonal festivals celebrated Dionysus' reunion with the dead. He was associated with the theatre, and theatrical masks were used as cult objects. Singing and dancing were part of his rites, which appear to have been more uninhibited in Northern Greece than in the south. In Thrace, for example, the god was sometimes represented by a goat, which was torn to pieces and eaten by the god's followers.

Euripides' great play, the *Bacchae*, is devoted to Dionysus, and it conveys best the rapture, grandeur and beauty of the Dionysian cult.

---

the old harbour, merits a visit. A colossal marble *kouros* (the name for a nude male statue of the Archaic period) takes pride of place in the entrance. This serene and enigmatic work of the 6th century B.C. shows what may be the god Apollo carrying a ram. Look for a fine ivory lion's head from the same century which captures the animal spitting in fury, his whiskers all abristle.

Another head, this one from the 3rd century B.C., is of the young Dionysus. His cult was much practised on Thásos. A good deal of wine-drinking must have gone on, judging from the size of the wine measures on exhibit. They are shaped like modern wash basins, with an outlet at the bottom for pouring the correct quantity into a carrying vessel.

Behind the museum are remains of the agora or marketplace, once an impressive public monument.

Pay your respects to the **satyr** at the Silene Gate *(Péli Silinoú)* on your way out of town. Satyrs were the half-animal creatures who looked after the infant Dionysus. This one wears the soft boots of the tragic actor. Once gloriously virile, he is slightly less so these days, worn away by the thousands of women who have touched him in the hope of having children. He still looks pleasantly wanton, but a little tired around the eyes.

Only 2 kilometres away is MAKRIÁMMOS BEACH, literally "long sand", a luxurious holiday resort. For a small fee, anyone can use the well maintained facilities. There are provisions for tennis and volleyball, skin-diving, fishing and boating. The beach is magnificent and the sea darkens into Homeric shades of grape and indigo at sunset.

From Makriámmos you can set out on a circular tour of the island. It takes about four hours to go all the way round. Along the way, be sure to taste the famous Thasian honey and the so-called jam of figs or walnuts *(gliká tou koutalioú)*. This isn't jam at all, but an ambrosial conserve of whole green figs or whole green walnuts. You may see old ladies brewing up family supplies in giant cauldrons set over glowing logs in their back gardens.

First head south through forest to the hill village of PANAGÍA. Its springs are re-

putedly beneficial for kidney complaints, and there are interesting Byzantine objects in the modern church. Back on the coast at CHRISÍ AKTÍ, a good catch of fish means a feast of seafood at the waterfront *tavérna*. Netting is done at night using flare lanterns and *gri-grí*, three small boats towed by a mother ship. Swimming and snorkelling are particularly rewarding here.

Farther south again, in the bay of KÍNIRA, long, shallow waves are ideal for surfing. Ancient quarries were situated at ALIKÍ, in the south-east corner of the island. You can still see the marks of the quarrymen's tools in the glittering area of marble which remains. Devout nuns from the nearby convent of ARCHÁNGELOS will show you two hollows in a stone floor, supposedly made by Saint Luke when he knelt to pray here.

There are more excellent beaches towards the west, before POTÓS, where you can turn off to visit the hill town of THEOLÓGOS, the mediaeval capital of Thásos. LIMENÁRIA is a centre for the mining of iron and precious minerals. Continue along the west coast to SKÁLA PRÍNOU, the other port for ferries from the mainland and the last stop on this circuit. **63**

Thrace

(Thráki)

The dividing line between the provinces of Macedonia and Thrace is the River Néstos. Once you've crossed the border you'll notice that the landscape, with its sprinkling of minarets, grows increasingly "Eastern", and the stork population thickens. However, like Macedonia, Thrace is rich tobacco country.

You pass through XÁNTHI, a pleasant little town; then the road runs south-east and crosses a narrow causeway between lake Vistonís and the bay. The country is flat. Rushes bend mournfully in the marshes and a church stands mirrored in its own melancholy reflection. Yet not far away (along a road running from the easterly tip of the lake) is the cheerful beach of FANÁRI, with tourist accommodation and camping.

There is no reason to linger in KOMOTINÍ. The village of STRÍMNI, on a secondary road to the south, is one of several towns in Northern Greece that celebrates Women's Day (see p. 88). ÁRATOS has a strong Turkish flavour with its minaret and Turkish-style houses. Now the road sometimes skirts patches of flaring sunflowers. Oxen plough the fields.

The road continues through agricultural land to **Alexandroúpolis,** named after King Alexander, who visited the town in 1920 after its liberation from Ottoman rule. The wide main street runs beside the sea and within sight of a lighthouse, a local landmark. In the summer, ferries sail regularly to Kamariótisa, the port of Samothrace.

From Alexandroúpolis it is 38 kilometres to the Turkish border. The River Évros marks the frontier between the two countries, and the swamps and lakes in the region are rich in fish and birds, including rare species of geese and eagles.

Samothrace

(Samothráki)

Journey's end for this tour of Macedonia and Thrace is the island of Samothrace. For a thousand years, pilgrims made their way here to worship at a far earlier seat of holiness than Áthos. Samothrace is a place for gods rather than men. Wild goats leap in a forbidding landscape of rugged granite mountains, and the accessible beaches are dark and pebbly. The roads are too rough for ordinary cars. Rely instead on local transport.

The sea dividing Samothrace from the mainland often runs streaked with foam from northerly winds. There is only one port, the small harbour of Kamariótisa, 25 miles from Alexandroúpolis. Less than 4,000 people reside on the island.

The glory and renown of Samothrace was its cult of the Great Gods. The major figure was a Great Mother of pre-Greek origin called Axieros.

Samothrace remains a mysterious island, filled with memories of ancient rites to the Great Gods.

She was worshipped at sacred rocks. Her subordinate mate was a fertility god called Kadmilos. Included in the worship were Axiokersos and Axiokersa, sacred figures parallel to Hades and Persephone, the gods of the underworld. While religious practices at Samothrace remain shrouded in mystery, some understanding of them is necessary to make a visit worthwhile. Membership was open to anyone—men, women and children of any nationality, both freemen and slaves. Elaborate initiation ceremonies took place, probably at night. There were two stages of initiation, the second involving confession, purification and a moral decision to lead a "better" life. The ritual language for many centuries was the Thracian tongue of the island's early inhabitants.

Both Aristophanes and Plato are understood to have joined. Philip II of Macedonia was initiated. In fact he met his wife Olympias, who later became the mother of Alexander, on Samothrace. Herodotus, the Greek historian, and many Romans revered the place. But the Emperor Hadrian was the last royal visitor. Christianity spread, and towards the end of the 4th century Samothrace lost its importance.

To visit the ancient shrine, take a taxi from the port of KAMARIÓTISA inland to nearby PALEÓPOLIS and ask at the hotel there for admittance. It is a short walk from the hotel to the **archaeological site.**

The first building you see is the **Anáktoron,** an initiation hall dating from about 500 B.C. Attached to it is a small room where members probably received a certificate of their initiation. The Arsinóion near by, built of Thasian marble and dedicated to the Great Gods in the 3rd century B.C. by the Egyptian Queen Arsinoe, was the largest circular building in ancient Greece. The altar is one of the oldest places in the sanctuary.

Farther south is a sacred rock of blue-green porphyry, where libations were poured. The **Témenos** (4th century B.C.), an enclosed courtyard, was probably used for feasts. Part of its frieze of musicians and dancing maidens is in the local museum. Adjacent to it is the **Ierón,** where the final ceremony took place.

Little is left of the theatre, but on the hill above is a fountain where the great *Winged Victory of Samothrace* once stood. The statue, discovered by French archaeologists in 1863, is now in the Louvre in Paris.

The Paleópolis **museum** (*mousío*) contains finds from the site. There are votive offerings, a 3rd-century B.C. terracotta of Eros and a Victory of about 130 B.C. from the Ierón. Jewellery exhibits include magnetic rings which were thought to bind worshippers to the Great Mother. The frieze of charming dancing girls frozen in attitudes of swift and graceful movement was taken from the Témenos; it is known as the *Nymphs of Samothrace*.

While on the island, visit SAMOTHRÁKI (*Chóra*) village. It is a rather jolting trip from Paleópolis to this hill town where old men still wear baggy "mountain trousers". You can go up to the Genoese fort here. (Ask a village youngster to show you the way.) Climbing enthusiasts may want to ascend **Mount Fengári**, at 5,250 feet the highest point in the Aegean. This is described in the *Iliad* as the "topmost peak of wooded Samothrace", from which Poseidon watched the battle of Troy. Take a local guide along on the five-hour climb.

There is a spa at THÉRMI, 20 minutes by taxi from Paleópolis. You bathe in waters supposedly good for fertility, the women's pool being considerably hotter than the men's.

West of Salonica

Pélla, Édessa, Lefkádia, Véria and Vergína can all be taken in on a long one-day trip from Salonica. If you have to make a choice, then settle for Pélla, one of Northern Greece's major archaeological sites.

Pélla

A few columns rise from the broken stumps of once-proud buildings to mark the site of Macedonia's ancient capital city, 38 kilometres north-west of Salonica. This was the seat of Macedonian kings from the time of Archelaus to the defeat of Perseus by the Romans. Alexander was born here, Aristotle walked the streets, and it was in Pélla that Euripides saw the première of his great play, the *Bacchae*. It is strange that the city should have vanished so completely and for so long.

Excavations were started in 1914, soon after the liberation of Macedonia. They were interrupted during the troubled period which followed, and popular belief had it that the town was well and truly buried. Then in 1957, a farmer digging out a cellar for his house came upon a marble Ionic capital. He informed the authorities, and Greece looked north in high excitement as serious **67**

WEST OF SALONICA

archaeological work began. Finds were almost immediate for, in fact, much of Pélla was only three to four feet down.

To date digging has uncovered wide streets, a highly evolved water purification and supply system and the remains of fine colonnaded buildings. Some of them must have been huge, as roof tiles up to three feet long have been found. They were stamped with the name of the city, an indisputable proof of its identity. It was known in advance that any transportable objects of value would be missing. These were carted off to grace Roman mansions together with the stone and marble blocks that have been used in local building over the centuries.

The archaeological site is a manageable size, with nothing to climb up, teeter along or fall off. So far the palace has not been identified with certainty. This would be the building constructed to the demanding taste of Archelaus and decorated with paintings by Zeuxis, one of the greatest artists of ancient Greece. Nor has the theatre been uncovered.

The remains that have come to light testify to the "Greekness" of Macedonia. This point of centuries-old friction has been hotly debated ever since the days of Demosthenes, when charges of "barbarianism" rose easily to the lips of Athenians. Discoveries also bear witness to the high level of artistic development in the up-

One of Pélla's famous mosaics shows a Macedonian lion hunt.

start north. This had long been under-rated, since contemporary accounts give little indication of the splendour of Macedonia.

Pride of Pélla is the **mosaics.** They are made of small river stones, a material rarely used in mosaic work. Skilful combinations of buff, ash-grey, white, red and honey-coloured pebbles give a three-dimensional quality. Outlines were generally worked with baked clay strips, although lead was sometimes used. The eyes were usually made of precious stones and have long since disappeared.

While the best of the mosaics are displayed in the local museum, some remain in their original places, including two geometric designs and floors where the pebbles are arranged freely, but not entirely at random. Borders are often stylized waves symbolizing Pélla's dependence on river, lake and sea, for in Alexander's day, the city was surrounded by extensive swampland, and there was a lake and a river, navigable all the way to the sea.

Pélla's delightful **museum** *(mousío)*, especially built to house finds, is situated just across the road from the site in a garden setting. There are many fine coins, tools, ves-

sels and figurines. Prominent among the sculpture is a marble dog sitting attentively on its back feet, faithful guardian of a tomb; the head of a young man, perhaps Alexander, judging by his heroic air; and a terracotta Athene in a horned helmet. The small bronze of Poseidon is a late Hellenistic copy of a larger work.

But the mosaics are the most splendid of the displays: Dionysus is wide-hipped, effeminate and shamelessly graceful on a bounding sacred panther. Some experts think that the celebrated *Lion Hunt* shows Craterus saving the life of his friend, Alexander.

Édessa

Édessa, 51 kilometres from Pélla, is backed by the foothills of Mount Vérmion. Many quicksilver streams chatter through the town, cooling the air and thickening vegetation. Most visitors come here to see the **cascades** which unite these waterways into a huge outpouring of thunder and foam, dropping from spray-spangled cliffs to the plain below.

Édessa's falls are impressive, but it is rather difficult walking on the muddy path leading down to them. You can stand right underneath, cut off from the world by a curtain of white

water. There is a tiny cave near by with some battered stalac-mites, but you will probably find greater enjoyment in the park at the top of the falls, where plane trees impose their gigantic, moisture-fed presence. There is a restaurant here, too, set near yet another foaming brook.

Lefkádia

The hamlet of Lefkádia, 18 kilometres to the south of Édessa, is the third place you visit on this triangle-shaped tour itinerary. There are several Macedonian tombs in the area, seemingly isolated one from another. But they were, in fact, part of a large cemetery connected to the site of the ancient town of MIÉZA close by. The most splendid of them is known as the "Great Tomb". The guard holds keys to the other tombs, but make sure you arrive at the site before 1.30 or after 4 p.m.

As a general rule, under-ground tombs uncovered in Macedonia are built of lime-stone and comprise one or two rooms housing family remains. Tombs were built and richly

Sheep rearing is important on the wide plains and uplands. **71**

decorated at great expense, then promptly buried, hidden from mortals and visible only to the gods in the underworld. The tumulus or mound of earth that covered them was planted with trees, and over the centuries their significance was forgotten.

The **Great Tomb** (*Mégas Táfos*) is also called the "Tomb of the Judgement". Its decoration is sagely protected from the elements by what looks like a small but sturdy aircraft hangar. The limestone edifice comprises two rooms of two stories and dates from the 3rd century B.C. Four frescoes on the walls of the first storey, applied while the plaster was still damp, depict the judgement of the dead man, who was obviously past middle age. He was probably a soldier, although the fact that he is shown without helmet or shield makes it clear that he did not actually die in battle.

There is also a frieze with scenes of Greeks fighting barbarians. This suggests that the dead man took part in battles in Asia, doubtless as a superior officer. Another frieze shows a mythical contest between the Centaurs and the Lapiths—a popular artistic subject depicting a brawl following a wedding feast at which the Centaurs, half man, half horse, had a drop too much and raped all the women, starting with the bride.

Véria

Lush trees border the road from Lefkádia to Véria, a distance of 18 kilometres. You pass through rich fruit-growing country and the prosperous town of NÁOUSA, famed for its plump peaches and full-bodied red wine. Véria itself is situated on the eastern slope of Mount Vérmion (you ski there in winter), and there are some fine views from the heights.

A pretty stream runs through the town, a tributary of the River Aliákmon, but the main point of interest is the so-called **Saint Paul Steps** (*Víma tou Ágiou Pávlou*). For Véria is the Berea of the New Testament, where Paul preached to Jews "more noble than those in Thessalonica" (*Acts 17: 10–14*). His Thessalonian opponents did not give him much time with these eager converts, however, but came and "stirred up the people". Paul left for the coast, where he took a ship to Athens, while Silas and Timothy stayed behind to organize the church.

A modern mosaic monument marks the supposed spot of the Apostle's preaching.

Vergína

Just 11 kilometres beyond Véria is Vergína, site of Aegae, the ancient capital of Macedonia before Pélla, and a sacred place afterwards. Macedonian kings were always buried here. In fact, a Delphic prophecy warned that the monarchy would crumble if its kings were buried anywhere else.

Excavations are going on south-east of town at the 4th-century B.C. royal tomb discovered intact in 1977 and not yet thought to be open to visitors. It is thought to be the grave of Philip II, stabbed to death at Aegae in 336 B.C. by a former guardsman. The unhappy event had been predicted by the Delphic prophecy, "Crowned to the altar comes the Bull; the Sacrificer stands". No one knows for sure if the oracle was an accomplice in this Macedonian murder mystery, but there can be no doubt about the magnificence of Philip's burial.

All transportable funerary objects have been removed to the Archaeological Museum in Salonica, where they are now on display (see p. 39). The unique fresco paintings that decorate the tomb inside and out are undergoing tests and cleaning before being shown to the public.

Excursions

Metéora

Metéora is across the Macedonian border in the province of Thessaly. Guided tours lasting two days take you there from Salonica. If driving, you follow the Salonica–Athens motorway to LÁRISA, turn inland to TRÍKALA, then head north again briefly to KALAMBÁKA. Allow five hours for the journey. By bus, you change at Lárisa.

Weathered monasteries perch like giant eagles' nests on a collection of barren rocks in the Valley of Metéora. The very name speaks of things beyond, hovering in the air, otherworldly. The origins of monastic life at Metéora go back to the 11th century, when monks lived in caverns at the foot of the rocks. Later they were driven to seek refuge from the Turks and Albanians on the heights. By the 16th century, there were 24 monasteries. Only a few are inhabited today, reminders of a faith and an asceticism so strong that it is hard for a modern visitor to comprehend.

There is no accommodation near the rocks. You can stay in

Kalambáka township or the nearby village of KASTRÁKI, and from there take the good road that leads to the weird group of masses and cones that tower above the valley. They were formed, as far as is known, from stones, sand and mud carried by river water into a lake and left there when river and lake receded. Wind, rain and earthquakes have scoured them to their present forms.

No one really knows how the first monks succeeded in climbing them. There are miraculous stories of kites, strings attached to a falcon's foot, the use of scaffolding and ascent via the tops of tall trees such as

still grow in the shadowy valleys. Possibly the goatherds and hunters in Kalambáka (or Stági, as it was then) were acquainted with ways and means.

Rope ladders became the accepted method, replaced later by a net suspended from a rope wound up by a hand winch. It took half an hour for visitors to reach some of the higher peaks by this method.

She nourishes pilgrims, body and soul: Metéora's monasteries are perched high like eyries, remote and isolated from the noisy, everyday world.

You can still see the equipment but nobody nowadays asks to try it out... Now there are power winches for hauling up supplies, and steps for human comings and goings.

Of the few monasteries left inhabited, three are commonly visited: Ágios Stéfanos (now a convent and orphanage), Megísti Meteóron and Ósios Varlaám. Megísti Meteóron and Ósios Varlaám have the most to offer in the way of late Byzantine frescoes, icons and wood-carvings. Ágios Stéfanos is the easiest to reach, since it is connected to the road by a footbridge. For the others you have to climb steep stone staircases.

The monasteries are very strict about visitors' clothing, and the car park is full of tourists doing quick change acts. Men, women and children are expected to wear at least elbow-length sleeves, men long trousers and women skirts. On the other hand, the monks (and nuns) are haphazard about opening hours, so make sure the monasteries will be open when you plan to visit them.

Megísti Meteóron or Metamórfosis (Monastery of the Transfiguration) was founded by Athanasius the Meteorite in the 14th century. It crowns the highest of the rocks, a flat-topped giant with a large summit some 2,000 feet above sea level. In spite of the catastrophes the monastery has suffered, it still preserves many beautiful works of Byzantine art, including ecclesiastical embroidery and wall paintings. The iconostasis in the lovely main church is rich with gilding and jewel-like icons.

Ósios Varlaám, adjacent to the Megísti Meteóron, is set almost as high, but on a smaller area. You mount 195 steps and pass through a gateway into a monastery garden full of flowers, butterflies and sunlight. Inside are more Byzantine works. Pause for a moment at the picture of a holy man lamenting earthly vanity over Alexander the Great's skeleton and remember that without Alexander's conquests and the subsequent spread of the Greek language, the Christian ethos would have encountered far more obstacles on its passage west.

Ágios Stéfanos is notable for its views of Kalambáka, glimmering in the distance like an oasis, and the wide plain of Thessaly stretching ahead. But the most magnificent scenery is provided by the rocks themselves, a stone forest mysterious by day, enormous and eerie by night.

Kastoriá

Charming, prosperous Kastoriá owes its name to the beaver, its prosperity to a flourishing fur industry and its charm to a lakeside situation on a pleasant promontory. There is an airport, and reliable bus and rail services link Kastoriá to Salonica, 210 kilometres away. A question that may be asked, however, is why such a booming town should have such poor streets and footpaths.

Legend has it that the town was founded by Orestes, son of Agamemnon, whose name graces the placid lake. Kastoriá was once strongly fortified against Albanian invasions, but there are few remaining signs of this. A road round the promontory offers pleasant views of the lake with flat-bottomed boats putting out to catch trout and other fresh-water fish. It seems just the place to take the perfect postcard picture or escape from an excess of Macedonian sun.

Kastoriá has dozens of churches, many of which are basilicas. This form stayed in local favour long after the Greek cross had taken over elsewhere. The most rewarding of the town's churches is to be seen at the **Panagía Mavriótissa** monastery, half-way round the lake on the south shore.

The church stands a few yards back from the lakeside road near a gigantic plane tree. The story that the tree is the same age as the 11th-century church is hardly to be taken literally, but it is certainly very old. The 12th-century frescoes that decorate the building reach from ground to roofline on the outside wall around the entrance and entirely cover the interior. Very much worth noticing, too, are the interior doors with their splendid carving.

Take time to visit the old house opposite (ask at the church), an example of Kastoriá's 17th- and 18th-century patrician residences, known as *archontiká*. Stout beams support a projecting storey with overhanging roof, small-paned windows and dark wooden shutters. The interior is equally restrained with its white plaster walls, solid woodwork and long platforms for sleeping.

Kastoriá is one of the few places where some of these houses remain intact. Others can be seen on the southern lakefront, closer to the centre of town. The most celebrated of them is the **Nátsi house,** decorated inside with imaginative ornamental frescoes.

You will probably have noticed that Kastoriá is full of

fur (hair-raising news for the asthmatic or the allergic). The industry that began with the local beaver colony has grown to international proportions, and many of the old *archontiká* have basements given over to the skin trade. Now pelts are imported and worked into garments that are sold worldwide,

and a fur fair at the end of March brings buyers from the four corners of the globe to Kastoriá.

You can buy furs cheaper here than almost anywhere in the world, and every few yards there's a shop for choosing your new mink, fox, squirrel or whatever. What you spend travelling here you more than save on a purchase, for the goods are already more expensive by the time they reach Salonica (see p. 84).

Outside Kastoriá, you will find good accommodation with swimming near DISPILIÓ, 7 kilometres around the lake, but bathing looks rather chilly, especially if you have seen the warm sands of Halkidiki.

From here, you can go on to the PRÉSPA lakes on the Yugoslav and Albanian borders. Not many tourists travel here, although there is good (if cool) swimming and an abundance of bird-life in the marshes. Superb pine forests clothe the high mountains near the Albanian border, and bears lumber peacefully through the thick woods—happily unconscious of all that is going on in Kastoriá.

Splendid Byzantine domes rise in Kastoriá, the lakeside town.

What to Do

Sports

Put the word "northern" out of your mind. From May to October, Halkidiki and the Aegean coast bask in a hot sun. The sea is blue and very clean. You can sunbathe, swim, boat and fish, or engage in an endless variety of water-sports. There is good riding year-round. Out of season, you can go hiking or climbing in the Vérmion and Pangéon mountains, and in winter, skiing at Mount Vérmion is an interesting possibility. For details on sports clubs and centres, see p. 121.

Beaches and Swimming

Northern Greece is blessed with plenty of long, sandy beaches and crystal-clear water. You can opt for the total privacy of a deserted cove or mingle with fellow holidaymakers and Greeks alike at organized beaches. For a small admission these provide every facility for dawn to dusk indulgence in water-sports and beach activities.

There are hired canoes and pedalos, tennis and volleyball courts, showers and dressing rooms. Many have children's playgrounds and shops selling **79** small gear like flippers, masks and fishing lines. Both resort hotels and National Tourist Organization campsites often permit non-residents to use their recreational facilities for a small charge, and the beaches are likely to be equipped with a protective net against jellyfish.

The beaches closest to Salonica are at Peréa (22 km.), Néi Epivátes (24 km.), Agía Triáda (28 km.), Néa Mikanióna (32 km.) and Epanomís (35 km.). Good organized beaches are to be found around Kassándra. Apart from the big tourist complex at Pórto Carrás, Sithonía is much less developed and the beaches are smaller, though very good. Try to arrive with everything you need, as there are not many villages, shops or people. The sands are also inviting near Ouranoúpolis, just west of Kavála, and on Thásos island.

NB: Sunbathing and swimming in the nude are now considered punishable offences.

Snorkelling and Spear Fishing

There are strict rules regulating the use of scuba apparatus, but it is permitted—from sunrise to sunset for viewing fish only—in certain places. The best areas are various designated sites on Sithonía and down the east coast of Thásos. The rules are made to safeguard fish and antiquities. Divers who happen upon ancient objects are asked not to move them, but to notify the nearest port authority or police station.

Underwater fishing without scuba equipment is permitted everywhere, the exceptions being that swimmers under 18 are not allowed to use spear guns, and spear fishing is forbidden near organized beaches or inside ports.

Water-Skiing

Qualified instruction is available at Gerakína Beach, where a couple of speedboats tow skiers. There is skiing at Pallíni Beach, and classes, too. In addition, the boatmen give plenty of advice and encouragement. You can also waterski at Pórto Carrás and at some of the naval and sailing clubs.

Wind-Surfing

This sport is rapidly growing in popularity, and many people in the area have their own gear. You can hire equipment at Gerakína Beach, Pallíni Beach and elsewhere.

Fishing

There are still plenty of fish to catch in rivers, lakes and sea, and fishing is freely allowed. In seaside ports or lakefront towns you can arrange to accompany local fishermen. A *tavérna* keeper will examine your catch in a friendly fashion and probably agree to cook it for you. There is a lot of night fishing with flare lanterns.

Boating and Sailing

Sail the North Aegean in a fully manned yacht, or captain yourself from port to port. This is a seafaring region and there are countless hire possibilities. Take lessons in sailing at the training school associated with the Kalamariá Naval Club in Salonica. The sailing club on the Salonica waterfront holds regattas during the summer season. You can hire a variety of small craft in most resort areas.

Riding

Non-members are admitted to the Northern Greece Riding Club in the Aretsoú area of Salonica, as well as to Ktíma Lítsa Riding Centre near Thérmi. There is also riding at Palíni Beach (Kalithéa), Sáni and Pórto Carrás.

Sure-footed, sturdy little local horses can be hired on Samothrace for exploring the island. The hotel at the archaeological site will help put you in touch with local guides.

Tennis

There are hard courts at all major beaches on Halkidikí, and the Salonica Tennis Club accepts non-members. Many National Tourist Organization beaches provide for tennis, and the Pórto Carrás complex, with 15 courts, should be popular with players. It's a good idea to bring your own racquet and balls.

Golf

The dedicated action of sprinklers and greensmen has produced an 18-hole golf course at Pórto Carrás. The greens, within sight of the sea, are freshened by salt breezes. Instruction is available.

Hiking and Mountain Climbing

Mount Vérmion and Mount Pangéon offer pleasant opportunities for walking and climbing in the late spring and early summer, when temperatures are mild and the wild flowers are at their best. The Greek Skiing and Alpine Association has organized mountain-refuge huts in these and some other localities. Ask at the National Tourist Organization Office in Salonica for information about altitudes, routes and accommodation available.

Exploring Samothrace on foot accompanied by a local youngster is the best way of getting to know the island. You can also climb Mount Fengári—arduous, but worth it for a view famed from antiquity.

Hunting

The forest of Sithonía is teeming with turtledoves, woodcock and quail. Partridge and hare are abundant both in the mountainous areas and open country of Northern Greece. Boar are to be found in the mountains.

Tourists are granted licences during the season, which runs from late August to early February. For full information about licences, bag limits and specific dates for the shooting of each kind of game, contact the Hunting Federation in Salonica or Alexandroúpolis.

Skiing

There is little in the way of winter sports in Northern Greece, but you can ski in the winter at Mount Vérmion, 28 kilometres from Véria. Séli, the main resort, has a small inn. There is a chair-lift.

The Greek sun you've been waiting for, combined to perfection with sea and sand at Gerakíni beach.

Shopping

Everything offered in a modern European city can be bought in Salonica. Prices are not much lower than in other countries, but you may be attracted by goods in cotton and cotton-synthetic fibre mixtures that are well-suited to the climate. Salonica's fashionable shops line Agía Sofías. For markets in the city, see p. 38.

You'll get most fun, though, out of shopping in the market area—whether for items of food to take home (herbs and cheeses are good choices) or for more particularly Greek souvenirs like the brass and copper items for which the city has long been famous and behind which lie centuries of tradition. But take a good look round at what's on offer before you buy—there's endless choice, but quality and prices both vary. Don't hesitate to pass over what you don't want. There'll be something else around the corner.

Most shops open from 8 a.m. to 2.30 p.m. on Monday, Wednesday and Saturday. Other days they close at 1.30 p.m. and re-open from 5 till about 8.30 p.m. All shops in Salonica open only from 7.30 a.m. to 2.30 p.m. in July.

Best Buys

Books. Salonica bookshops have excellent selections of publications on various aspects of the area in many languages. Whether your interest is Byzantine churches, Greek cookery or the life of Alexander the Great, you'll find something of interest. Occasionally, the local translation lets the author down, and you'll be more enthralled by the spelling than the text. Greek museum and archaeological publications are very fine.

Brass and Copper. For brass and copper ware, head for the church of Panagía Chalkéon in Salonica. The street of the coppersmiths runs just alongside and there's a dazzling choice of both decorative and functional items.

Furs. The fur workshops in Kastoriá supply the rest of Greece and send garments all over the world. Prices are comparatively low, dropping still further in the summer months. The choice is extensive: Along with coats, stoles, hats and gloves, there are floor and bed rugs, many of them in a "patchwork" style.

A more limited selection at higher prices is available in Salonica and throughout the area, but it can be worth your while to make a trip to Kastoriá simply to buy a fur. Resist pressure and take your time. Quality is available if you know what you are looking for, and there are plenty of fun furs as well.

Honey and Foodstuffs. On Thásos there is fine honey, and the tins of fig and walnut conserve are a sweet treat (see p. 63). Greek olive oil is another delicious bargain. These items are all worth carrying home if you can find a convenient means of transporting them.

Icons. Selecting an authentic icon is a tricky business. Study examples of these religious images in churches and museums, and make sure you buy from a reputable dealer. You must have government permission to export originals. Keep in mind that icon smuggling is a serious offence.

Brass and copper utensils dazzle the eye and entice shoppers to the Street of the Coppersmiths.

Reproductions of Byzantine art are also available. There are specialist shops in Salonica at the Rotunda end of the Odós Egnatía. On Halkidiki nuns in a convent near the village of Ormília (off the main road between Kassándra and Sithonía) sell icons they paint in their own workshops (as well as handwoven carpets). They enjoy having visitors and may even show you around their community. Mount Áthos monks also sell votive paintings in keeping with the spirit of the Byzantine tradition.

Rugs and Woollen Goods. Arnéa is the wool town. Here you can find handmade *flokáti* rugs of pure wool and woven carpets with traditional designs. Also for sale is a range of knitted articles including heavy, creamy-white sweaters. These goods are available elsewhere, but there is naturally a better selection on the spot, and prices are lower, too.

Souvenirs. Those ubiquitous

Ronald Mc Leod

Entertainment

There's plenty to do at night in Northern Greece, with a choice of both traditional Greek and sophisticated international entertainments. From Salonica the night-owls go to discotheques at Aretsoú, a waterside suburb. More discotheques are to be found at the tourist resorts on Halkidikí; those dotted around Kassándra are in the open air. (Note that both nightclubs and discos must close by 2 a.m.)

A happy mixture of tourists and Greeks always gathers at *tavérnes*, and, sooner or later, traditional dancing begins. You'll quickly pick up the steps of the inevitable but nonetheless compelling *sirtáki*, a group dance, and recognize the sound of the *bouzoúki*, the eight-stringed mandolin which has stretched its name to include all Greek song and dance. (Note that some resort hotels offer lessons in Greek dancing.) Some *bouzoúki* (or *rebétiko*) songs are now internationally well known thanks to the music of Manos Hadjidakis and Mikis Theodorakis, the singing of Nana Mouskouri and the films of Melina Mercouri.

In remoter villages you may be lucky enough to happen on traditional dancing at a local

"Greek art" shops sell cotton goods, worry beads *(komboloia)*—not widely used in the north—olive-wood articles, postcards (and stamps), rugs and general souvenirs. Thásos specializes in objects featuring a supremely virile satyr.

Wine. Bottles of Château Carrás and Boutári wine are worth taking home to share with friends in memory of your Greek holiday. Remember the import restrictions at your country of destination.

fête. The ancient and ever-popular *sirtós* (dragging dance) portrayed so often in classical vase paintings may already be familiar to you. It was probably first performed around the altar during pagan rituals, and both men and women take part. The *pidiktós* (leaping dance) is sometimes seen in Northern Greece. A popular group of dances called *boúles* are performed in Náousa on the last Sunday of carnival. These dances came to symbolize the struggle for liberation when Greek soldiers fighting in the revolution disguised themselves in women's clothing to slip home unrecognized during carnival. Then as now, the *boúles* were an important part of the celebration.

There is a state theatrical company in Salonica, the Northern Greece National Theatre. In summer, the group performs festival programmes put on by the National Tourist Organization. These are staged in Salonica and at the old theatres of Philippi and Thásos (see p. 90).

Costumed Macedonian girls poised to throw flowers during a presidential visit, a custom that Alexander the Great certainly would have approved.

Calendar of Events

Northern Greece celebrates the usual national holy days and holidays, as well as some festivals mentioned here.

January 8

Women's Day — Still observed at Monoklisiá and Néa Pétra near Sérres and in the Thracian village of Strímni near Komotiní. The men stay home while the women carouse in the streets and *tavérnes*. The festival is descended from Dionysian fertility rites.

February

Carnival — During the three weeks before Lent, there are carnival celebrations in the streets of Salonica. On the last Sunday before Lent, bonfires are lighted in the village squares of western Macedonia.

March/April

Orthodox Good Friday and Easter — Candlelit funeral processions with a flower-bedecked bier pass through the streets at night. Midnight services on Holy Saturday announce Christ is risen. The paschal candle is lighted, church bells peal and fireworks illuminate the sky. Easter Sunday is celebrated with a traditional meal of roast lamb and eggs dyed red.

Kastoriá Fur Show — One week towards the end of March when international buyers flock in.

May

Feast of Saint Constantine and Saint Helen — In Lagadás, Agía Eléni and Ágios Pétros, on May 21 and possibly for a day or two afterwards, there is a ritual fire-walking ceremony (see box, p. 91).

June

Navy Week — There are fireworks and displays on or near the harbour in Salonica towards the end of June or the beginning of July.

July/August

Wine festival Wine is free of charge at the National Tourist Organization campsite in Alexandroúpolis from the beginning of July to mid-August. Folk dances and songs. Local bus from Alexandroúpolis.

Drama festival Presentation of classical drama in the ancient theatres of Thásos and Philippi. Two weeks in August.

September

International Trade Fair National and international merchandise is on display in Salonica.

Song and Film festivals Both the Greek Light Song Festival and the Greek Film Festival take place after the fair in the theatre of the Association of Macedonian Studies.

October

Demetria Festival A series of cultural programmes presented in Salonica by Greek and visiting companies. This is the revival of a Byzantine tradition.

Ordeal by Fire

The Feast of Saint Constantine and Saint Helen commemorates a miraculous event. The story goes that once, in the Eastern Thracian village of Kostí, a church dedicated to Saint Constantine caught fire. The icons were heard to groan aloud, and some of the villagers braved the flames to rescue them. They emerged from the fire unscathed.

Every year since, worshippers clutching icons work themselves into a trance and walk or dance on smouldering ashes, apparently unhurt. They give out short gasps, hence their name, *anastenárides* (from *anastenázo*—to sigh). Nowadays, the firewalking is performed in Lagadás by descendants of refugees from Kostí. The ceremony is accompanied by drinking.

The festival probably has its origin in Dionysian rites, rather than in Christianity. In fact, the celebrations are not always approved by the Orthodox Church and have been much subdued in recent years.

Traditionally a "perfect" (ungelded) bull is sacrificed. In the old days, the hide was cut into pieces and every family was given a pair of sandals made from it.

Wining and Dining

Northern Greece has all the ingredients of a fine cuisine. There is plenty of fresh fish in the coastal areas, orchards around Náousa yield a generous variety of fruit and vineyards on Sithonía produce some of the best wines in the country. Food is slightly richer and more spicy, owing to the influence of Balkan and Turkish cooking, but most of the familiar Greek dishes are available.

Cooks excel in pastry-making. Pies of spinach *(spanakópita)*, vegetables *(chortópita)* and cheese *(tirópita)* are a Greek speciality popular in Salonica. A lot of meat is eaten, especially goat in the villages. From September to May you may be lucky enough to sample game *(kinígi)* in a hunting area. *Lagós stifádo*, hare braised with pearl onions in a tomato sauce, is one of many unusual regional dishes. All in all, eating in the north is a very satisfying experience.*

With so many restaurants and *tavérnes* to choose from, you won't want to be restricted

---

* For more information on wining and dining in Greece, consult the Berlitz EUROPEAN MENU READER.

to the international fare of the tourist hotels. In Salonica, the best eating places are to be found along the waterfront from Platía Aristotélous to the White Tower, as well as in the area of the old town up to the Kástra and the Eptapírgio. Out of town, you can enjoy fine food at the waterside suburbs of Aretsoú, Peréa and Néa Kríni. The food in the *tavérnes* of Panórama, a hilly suburb, is as pleasant as the view. Here, as elsewhere in Greece, dining is out-of-doors whenever possible.

Throughout Greece lunch is traditionally served late and you seldom sit down to dinner before 8 at the earliest. No one objects in the least if you linger on till after midnight—restaurants stay open until 2 a.m. In smaller places, don't forget the

Daylight or candlelight, expect only the best in Northern Greece.

engaging habit of wandering into the kitchen to see for yourself what's going on. It's often easier to choose from the dishes simmering on the stove than to order from the menu.

All eating establishments (except those in the luxury class) are price-controlled according to category. The service charge is included in the bill, but you should leave a little extra for the waiter. To catch his attention, simply call out "parakaló" (please).

Greek Specialities

Here is a sample of typical dishes found throughout the country:

Dolmádes. Vine leaves stuffed with seasoned rice or meat, served cold as an hors d'œuvre or hot with *avgolémono*, a tangy sauce.

Dzadzíki. A dip of yoghurt, cucumber and crushed garlic eaten with that fine, honest stuff, Greek bread.

Kalamarákia. Small squid fried in batter.

Keftédes. Meatballs, usually of minced beef and lamb, with grated onion, cinnamon, crushed mint leaves and oregano. They're baked or deep-fried in oil.

Kolokíthia gemistá me rízi ke kimá. Baby marrows (zucchini) stuffed with rice and minced meat.

Mousaká. Baked layers of aubergine (eggplant) and minced meat with a white sauce and grated cheese.

Psarósoupa. A fisherman's soup, much like French *bouillabaisse*. A variation is *kakaviá*, made with small fish, onions, carrots, potatoes and olive oil.

Taramosaláta. A creamy fish-egg paste used as a dip. Lemon and black pepper enhance the flavour.

Fish and Seafood

Aegean waters supply northern coastal towns with a wealth of fish and seafood, while freshwater fish is available inland in lakeside areas. Fish in Greece (not cheap) is usually grilled or fried, basted with oil and served with lemon juice.

The kind depends on the catch of the day:

Astakós. Lobster-like crayfish (minus claws), often served with oil and lemon sauce or garlic mayonnaise. Expensive.

Barboúni. Red mullet, a delicacy for Greeks. Usually fried.

Chtapódi. Octopus, usually boiled or cut in slices and fried.

Garídes. Shrimp.

Glóssa. Sole, rare but delicious.

Karavídes. Spiny lobster.

Kéfalos. Grey mullet.

Mídia. Mussels, served warm, truly delicious.

Sfirída. Whiting, may be served whole or in slices.

Sinagrída. Red snapper, usually served whole.

Xifías. Swordfish, sometimes flavoured with oregano and grilled on a skewer.

Meat Dishes

Even the simplest restaurant can do an honourable job with veal, lamb or pork chops. Pieces of meat are delicious when skewered and grilled over charcoal; ask for *souvláki*. Also good is spit-roasted chicken, *kotópoulo psitó sti soúvla*. *Donér kebáb*, a cone of sizzling lamb or other meat roasted on a revolving spit, is a speciality of snack vendors. As the meat cooks, slices are cut from the outside. In *pastítsio*, minced meat and pasta are prepared in the same way as *mousaká* (see above). Tripe soup *(patsás)* is particularly well-cooked in Salonica, and it is worth seeking out those restaurants that feature it.

Other Courses

Healthy and colourful is the *saláta choriátiki,* the typical salad of tomatoes, cucumber, green pepper, *féta* cheese and olives. If you prefer, you can order any of these items separately.

Vegetables are usually cooked in olive oil *(laderá).* Marrows, tomatoes, peppers and aubergines (eggplant) can be served stuffed with rice *(gemistá).* Okra *(bámies)* is particularly delicious.

The countryside is full to overflowing with fruit. Cherries come to the table in little bowls of iced water, and in out-of-the-way places, you may have

Whether the fruit of the earth or the beasts of the field, the accent is on tasty specialities.

the chance to taste the dark and almondy wild variety. There is an abundance of peaches, apricots, nectarines, figs and melons, too.

Foremost among Greek cheeses *(tirí)* is the ubiquitous *féta*, made of goat's or sheep's milk. You will also encounter the mild and yellow gruyère-like *graviéra; kaséri,* light yellow with a soft texture; and *kefalotíri,* very strong and salty. *Manoúri,* a kind of fresh whey cheese, is often mixed with honey as a dessert.

Sweets

Salonica shops specializing in chocolates and chocolate cakes could hold their own anywhere. Try the tempting *kariókes* and *karré nouá.* The *trígonas,* or horn-shaped pastries of Panórama, make one very good reason for visiting that hillside town. Honey-flavoured sweets baked in a pan and steeped in syrup are as popular in the north as they are in the rest of Greece. Among them are *baklavás,* paper-thin pastry filled with chopped nuts and *kataífi,* a shredded pastry wrapped around almonds and walnuts.

Graníta, a water-ice with fruit syrup, often proves more refreshing than ordinary ice-cream on a hot summer's day.

Fruit preserves in heavy syrup *(gliká tou koutalioú)* are served in cafés and almost every Greek home. This traditional dessert is presented in a little bowl and accompanied by a glass of water. But the nicest sweet of all may well be natural yoghurt *(giaoúrti)* topped with honey *(méli),* especially if it's fresh from a village dairy.

Drinks

A holiday in Northern Greece would not be complete without paying due respect to a bottle of Château Carrás. There are two whites, including a good *blanc de blanc,* a rosé and two reds. Of considerable merit is Boutári, from the area near Mount Vérmion. This full-bodied red is not unlike a Châteauneuf du Pape. Other wines worth trying are Tsántalis, Makedonikó (white), Áthos (white and rosé), Agiorítiko (red). A very good selection of wines of the local Cooperative Wine Producers are also available.

Apart from these there is *rétsina,* a white wine flavoured with pine resin. Despite the taste—similar to turpentine although not as strong—Greeks claim that it aids the digestion of rich, oily foods. The reason that the resin is added is to retain the wine's distinctive taste, originally acquired from the pine-wood casks sealed with resin that used to be used for shipping. Deméstica, red or white, is a reliable choice.

Oúzo, by now an international apéritif, is distilled from crushed vine stems and has an aniseed flavour. It is drunk neat *(skéto)*, on the rocks *(me págo)* or with water. *Mezédes* or cocktail snacks automatically accompany it at no extra charge. Olives, *féta* cheese, *taramosaláta*, octopus and tomato slices are the usual offerings. Sample all this in a special café, the *ouzéri*.

The beer *(bíra)*, heavier than lager, is good and refreshing. Greek brandy is pleasant but does not rival French cognac. Metaxá is the best-known brand; Kambá is a little drier.

If you prefer, cola drinks are always available, as well as bottled orange and lemon squash *(portokaláda, lemonáda)*. Tea is a perfectly recognizable, acceptable table beverage.

Traditional Greek coffee, served in a *demi-tasse*, comes sweet *(éna varí glikó)*, medium *(éna métrio)*, slightly sweet *(éna me olíghi)* or without sugar *(éna skéto)*. A glass of water usually accompanies it. Iced coffee, very refreshing, is graced with a French name: *kafé frappé*. Espresso coffee is catching on, but your breakfast cup is likely to be of the powdered variety.

To Help You Order

Could we have a table?

Tha boraúsame na échoume éna trapézi?

I'd like a/an/some…

Tha íthela…

beer	**mía bíra**	milk	**gála**
bread	**psomí**	mineral water	**metallikó neró**
coffee	**éna kafé**	potatoes	**patátes**
cutlery	**machero-**	rice	**rízi**
	pírouna	salad	**mía saláta**
dessert	**éna glikó**	soup	**mía soúpa**
fish	**psári**	sugar	**záchari**
fruit	**froúta**	tea	**éna tsái**
glass	**éna potíri**	(iced) water	**(pagoméno)**
ice-cream	**éna pagotó**		**neró**
meat	**kréas**	wine	**krasí**

97

How to Get There

If the choice of ways to go is bewildering, the complexity of fares and regulations can be downright stupefying. A reliable travel agent will have full details of all the latest possibilities, fares and regulations.

BY AIR

Scheduled flights

There are direct flights to Salonica from several major European cities. However, most regularly scheduled flights change in Athens for Salonica. Olympic Airways operate frequently each day between Athens and Salonica, about a 45-minute trip from the Greek capital. Kavála airport is mainly used for domestic flights to and from Athens, but also for international charter flights.

Charter flights and package tours

From the U.K. and Ireland: Package and "theme" holidays are available, many of them good value for money. A tour operator can also give details on "Wanderer" holidays for travellers planning a walking tour, using vouchers for accommodation in inexpensive youth hostels and boarding houses.

From North America: GIT's (Groupe Inclusive Tours) of 15 days or longer feature Salonica and Macedonia. Included in the progammes are airfare, all transfers, hotel accommodation throughout, sightseeing excursions, some or all meals, as well as a cruise to various Greek Isles and Turkey.

BY ROAD

The most direct route from Northern Europe is via Frankfurt–Munich–Graz (Austria)–Belgrade–Niš (Yugoslavia) and on to Salonica. Another possibility is to drive through France and Italy and take one of the Italy–Greece ferries and go on to Salonica via Athens: in summer, car-ferries operate frequently between certain Italian ports and Greece. The most popular routes are Brindisi–Patras and Venice–Piraeus.

BY RAIL

Through trains run from London via Ostend, Munich and Belgrade to Salonica. There is also a route from Paris via Bologna, Brindisi and Patras (the fare includes ferry crossing Brindisi–Patras).

Anyone under 26 can purchase an *Inter-Rail-Card* which allows one month of unlimited 2nd-class rail travel on all participating European railways. The *Rail Europ Senior Card* (obtainable before departure only) entitles senior citizens to buy train tickets for European destinations at reduced prices. Anyone living outside of Europe and North Africa can purchase a *Eurailpass* before leaving home. People intending to undertake a lot of rail travel in Greece may like to buy a *Greek Tourist Card* which is available for unlimited 2nd-class travel over the lines of the Greek Railways.

BY SEA

Cargo/passenger services are available from the U.S. to Piraeus in Greece. Departures are approximately three to four times per month with dates and ports-of-call subject to cargo requirements. Booking should be made well in advance.

There are also cargo/passenger services from Southampton to Piraeus. The duration of the voyage is approximately 10 days.

When to Go

Salonica can be stifling hot in summer and bitterly cold in winter, when the city is sometimes swept by the *Vardáris*, a wind that blows from the north-west. Light breezes temper the heat in sea-side areas, and the hill region of the Halkidiki mainland is pleasant in summer. July and August are the hottest months; February is the coldest.

Average monthly temperatures:

		J	F	M	A	M	J	J	A	S	O	N	D
Air temperature													
Max.	°F	50	52	59	65	77	87	91	91	83	74	61	54
	°C	10	11	15	20	25	30	32	32	28	23	16	12
Min.	°F	36	38	45	50	59	64	70	70	64	57	47	40
	°C	2	3	7	10	15	18	21	21	18	14	8	5
Water temperature													
	°F	55	55	57	61	65	74	77	77	74	66	61	57
	°C	13	13	14	16	20	23	25	25	23	19	16	14

Planning Your Budget

To give you an idea of what to expect, here are some average prices in Greek drachmas (drs.). However, due to inflation, they must be regarded as approximate.

Airport transfer. Taxi to Salonica centre 400 drs., coaches 45 drs.

Baby-sitters. 450–500 drs. per hour.

Bicycle hire. About 500–600 drs. per day.

Camping (per day). 450–500 drs. per person/car/tent/caravan (trailer), plus 6% tax.

Car hire (high season July–mid-Oct.). *Subaru, Suzuki* or similar 2,000 drs. per day, 25 drs. per km., 35,000 drs. per week with unlimited mileage. Add 20% tax.

Cigarettes. Greek brands 60 drs. for 20, foreign brands 100–180 drs.

City buses (within Salonica). 30 drs.

Entertainment. *Bouzoúki* (with one drink) 1,500–2,500 drs., discotheque (with one drink) 500–600 drs., cinema 200–250 drs.

Guides. 4,000 drs. for half day, 6,000 drs. for full day.

Hairdressers. *Woman's* haircut 1,200 drs., shampoo and set 1,000–1,600 drs., permanent wave 3,500 drs. *Man's* haircut 600–750 drs.

Hotels (double room with bath, half board). Class A 8,000 drs., class B 6,000 drs., class C 3,500–4,000 drs.

Meals and drinks. Continental breakfast 400 drs., lunch/dinner in fairly good establishment 1,200 drs., iced coffee 120 drs., *oúzo* 100 drs., soft drinks 85–160 drs., Greek brandy 100–120 drs.

Shopping bag. Bread (½ kg.) 40 drs., butter (250 g.) 120 drs., 6 eggs 90 drs., *féta* cheese (½ kg.) 450 drs., potatoes (1 kg.) 50 drs., minced meat (1 kg.) 650 drs., coffee (250 g.) 400 drs., soft drinks (small bottle) 50 drs.

Taxis. Meter starts at 45 drs., minimum charge 110 drs. Ride from Salonica to Agía Triáda 1,500 drs., to Pallíni Beach or Áthos Palace (on the Kassándra peninsula) 5,000 drs.

BLUEPRINT for a Perfect Trip

An A-Z Summary of Practical Information and Facts

Contents

A star (*) following an entry indicates that relevant prices are to be found on page 100.

Listed after some basic entries is the appropriate Greek expression, usually in the singular, plus a number of phrases that should help you when seeking assistance.

A **AIRPORT*** (ΑΕΡΟΔΡΟΜΙΟ—*aerodrómio*). Salonica has a modern international airport at Míkra, 15 kilometres from the centre of town. Olympic Airways (the national airline) links Salonica to Athens and the island of Límnos.

Within the airport building are car hire agencies, currency exchange booths and refreshment bars, as well as shops selling newspapers, magazines, books in various languages and souvenirs.

Helpful advice is freely dispensed in a multitude of languages at the information desk in the main foyer.

An Olympic Airways bus meets all Olympic flights and drops passengers off at the city terminal, but most passengers not on package tours (that are met by special coaches going directly to their hotels) choose to take a taxi from the stand right outside the airport terminal; the ride takes about 20–30 minutes. Porters are available.

Last-minute shopping can be done in the duty-free shop before flight departure.

Airport information: tel. (031) 411-977.

Olympic Airways office: Komninón 1; tel. (031) 260-121.

Flight information: (031) 261-221/2.

Porter!	**Achtofóre!**
Take these bags to the	**Pigénete aftés tis aposkevés**
bus/taxi, please.	**sto leoforío/taxí, parakaló.**

ALPHABET. See also LANGUAGE, and box on page 24. The exotic letters of the Greek alphabet needn't be a mystery to you. The table below lists the Greek letters in their capital and small forms, followed

102 by the letters they correspond to in English.

A α	a	as in bar	
B β	v		
Γ γ	g	as in go*	
Δ δ	d	like th in this	
E ε	e	as in get	
Z ζ	z		
H η	i	like ee in meet	
Θ θ	th	as in thin	
I ι	i	like ee in meet	
K κ	k		
Λ λ	l		
M μ	m		
N ν	n		

Ξ ξ	x	like ks in thanks	
O o	o	as in bone	
Π π	p		
P ρ	r		
Σ σ, ς	s	as in kiss	
T τ	t		
Y υ	i	like ee in meet	
Φ φ	f		
X χ	ch	as in Scottish loch	
Ψ ψ	ps	as in tipsy	
O/Ω ω	o	as in bone	
OY ου	ou	as in soup	

* except before i- and e-sounds, when it's pronounced like y in yes

ANTIQUITIES *(archéa)*. Export of antiquities and works of art found in the area is forbidden unless permission has been obtained from the Director of the Archaeological Museum of Salonica. Permission is not always granted. If it is, an export permit may then be requested from the Customs Office (see below). People caught trying to take artefacts out of Greece without official permission are subject to prosecution. They face a stiff fine and a prison sentence.

Main Customs Office: Odós Koundouriótou, Salonica, in the port; tel. (031) 521-502/531-220.

BEACHES. The National Tourist Organization runs a certain number of organized public beaches in various parts of the country. These offer facilities such as restaurants or snack bars, shops, bathing huts, children's playgrounds, tennis courts, canoes, pedalos, etc. All beaches are open daily from 8 a.m. to 7 p.m. and most function from April 1 to October 31. They charge minimal entrance fees.

Here's a listing for Northern Greece:

Alexandroúpolis Beach, Asproválta Beach, Fanári Beach, Kalamítsi Beach (Kavála), Kavála Beach, Thermaikoú Beach (at Agía Triáda; open all year round).

C

CAMPING* (ΚΑΜΠΙΝΓΚ—*"camping"*). Camping in Greece is permitted only at organized sites; there's no lack of these throughout the area. Campers will be impressed by the space, shade and cleanliness of the sites, as well as by the imagination that has gone into providing facilities.

Below is a list of localities with organized campsites in the area—open all year—run by the National Tourist Organization of Greece.

Agía Triáda, 28 km. south of Salonica.

Alexandroúpolis, 2 km. from town.

Asproválta, 85 km. east of Salonica on the road to Kavála.

Bátis, near Kavála.

Epanomí, 27 km. south of Salonica.

Fanári, 30 km. south-west of Komotiní.

Kriopigí, on Kassándra, Halkidiki; 107 km. south of Salonica.

Palioúri, on Kassándra, Halkidiki; 125 km. south of Salonica.

Some organized campsites are privately run. For a full list, contact the NTOG office in your home country, the EOT office in Salonica (see TOURIST INFORMATION OFFICES) or a local tourist police station. Most private sites are open from the beginning of April to end October.

Is there a campsite near by?	**Ipárchi éna méros giá "camping" edó kondá?**
We have a caravan (trailer).	**Échoume trochóspito.**

CAR HIRE* (ΕΝΟΙΚΙΑΣΕΙΣ ΑΥΤΟΚΙΝΗΤΩΝ—*enikiásis aftokiníton*). See also DRIVING IN GREECE. The main car hire firms have offices in Salonica. On Halkidiki, enquire at your hotel reception desk. Demand is high. If possible, reserve in advance. Car rental is expensive in Greece, but bargaining is sometimes possible with local firms.

The International Driving Permit is obligatory for all foreigners *hiring* a car in Greece but, in practice, firms accept virtually any national licence that has been held for at least one year. Some companies do not hire cars to drivers under 25.

I'd like to hire a car (tomorrow).	**Tha íthela na nikiáso éna aftokínito (ávrio).**
for one day/a week	**giá mía iméra/mía evdomáda**
Please include full insurance.	**Sas parakaló na simberilávete miktí asfália.**

CHILDREN*. It is no exaggeration to say that the Greeks adore children and seem to have found a happy middle road between freedom and discipline. Young children often go out with their parents in the evening and are accepted almost everywhere. Many of the Halkidiki hotels have children's swimming pools, and arrangements can be made for lessons. Gerakína Beach arranges special pool afternoons for youngsters, with supervised fun and races—and the nice thing is that everybody gets a prize.

If you need a baby-sitter, enquire at the hotel reception desk and arrangements will be made, providing you give sufficient warning. If you have taken accommodation in a private house, your Greek hosts will almost certainly solve the problem but, again, let them know in advance.

If your child strays, inform anyone around who speaks your language and go to the nearest policeman. Chances are that he or she will come off with nothing worse than a scare.

Can you get me/us a baby-sitter for tonight?	**Boríte na mou/mas vríte mía "baby-sitter" giapópse?**

CIGARETTES, CIGARS, TOBACCO* *(tsigára, poúra, kapnós)*. The sign to look for is ΚΑΠΝΟΠΩΛΕΙΟ *(kapnopolío)*. Greek tobacco products, of good quality and generally mild, are far cheaper than the foreign brands (some manufactured under licence in Greece) available. These may be hard to obtain, so buy supplies duty-free in your country (see ENTRY AND CUSTOMS REGULATIONS).

A packet of .../A box of matches, please.	**Éna pakéto .../Éna koutí spírta, parakaló.**
filter-tipped	**me fíltro**
without filter	**chorís fíltro**

CLOTHING. You'll need beach clothing, of course, and sunglasses, which tend to be expensive in resort boutiques. Bathing slippers are a good idea if you are going to Samothrace, where the beaches are stony. They are sold in beach shops throughout the area but are harder to find on Samothrace itself.

Greek town-dwellers wear light-weight city clothes throughout the summer months. Cotton is preferable to synthetics in hot weather,

C especially for underclothes. Women will have plenty of opportunity to dress up at night, and long skirts are not out of place. Women should take a light wrap and men a jacket or sweater for cool summer evenings.

Heavy clothes are a necessity in winter, when temperatures sometimes drop to near freezing.

Hotels discourage the use of their towels on the beach, so take your own for swimming and sunbathing.

COMMUNICATIONS

Post offices (ΤΑΧΥΔΡΟΜΕΙΟ—*tachidromío*) handle letters, stamp sales, parcels and money orders, but not telegrams and phone calls. They can be recognized by a yellow sign reading ΕΛ.ΤΑ.

Hours are usually from 8 a.m. to 8 p.m., Monday to Friday.

In tourist hotels, the reception desk will usually take care of despatching mail.

Registered letters and parcels going out of Greece are checked before being sent, so don't seal them until you have presented them at the post office desk.

Poste restante (general delivery). If you don't know ahead of time where you'll be staying, address your mail poste restante:

> Mr. John Smith
> Poste Restante
> Thessaloníki
> Greece

In Salonica, you can pick it up from the main post office at:

Tsimiskí 43-45, from 8.30 a.m. to 9 p.m.

Take your passport with you for identification.

Telegrams (*tilegráfima*) and **Telephone** (*tiléfono*). Every town of any size has an office of the Greek Telecommunications Organization—OTE—and this is where you go to telephone or send telegrams—if, that is, your hotel is too small to be able to cope. Tourist hotel staff are very helpful and, as well as putting your call through for you, take telephone messages and handle telex communications.

International trunk lines are often busy and you may have to wait up to two hours at peak times. Reverse-charge (collect) calls can be made (dial 151 for Europe and 161 for the rest of the world).

The main OTE office in Salonica is at Ermoú 48.

Telephone Spelling Code							
A	Aléxandros	H	Iraklís	N	Nikólaos	T	Timoléon
B	Vasílios	Θ	Theódoros	Ξ	Xenofón	Y	Ipsilántis
Γ	Geórgios	I	Ioánnis	O	Odisséfs	Φ	Fótios
Δ	Dimítrios	K	Konstantínos	Π	Periklís	X	Chrístos
E	Eléni	Λ	Leonídas	P	Ródos	Ψ	Psáltis
Z	Zoí	M	Menélaos	Σ	Sotírios	Ω	Oméga

Where's the (nearest) post office?	**Pou íne to kodinótero tachidromío?**
Have you received any mail for…?	**Échete grámmata giá…?**
A stamp for this letter/ postcard, please.	**Éna grammatósimo giaftó to grámma/kart postál, parakaló.**
express (special delivery)	**exprés**
airmail	**aeroporikós**
registered	**sistiméno**
I want to send a telegram to…	**Thélo na stílo éna tilegráfima sto…**
Can you get me this number in…?	**Boríte na mou párete aftó ton arithmó…?**
reverse-charge (collect) call	**plirotéo apó to paralípti**
personal (person-to-person) call	**prosopikí klísi**

COMPLAINTS. Either the proprietor of the establishment in question or your hotel manager, travel-agency representative or tour operator should be the first recourse for complaints. If you still aren't satisfied, go to the tourist police (see POLICE). Simply mentioning you intend doing so should bring results. Many disputes stem from small misunderstandings or linguistic problems. Rather than explode in anger, draw a deep breath and try to see things the Greek way—especially where time is involved.

CONSULATES *(proxenío)*

In Salonica:

Great Britain and Ireland: Venizélou 8; tel. (031) 278-006
British Council, Ethnikís Amínis 9; tel. (031) 235-236
South Africa: Leofóros Níkis 21; tel. (031) 234-133
U.S.A.: Leofóros Níkis 59; tel. (031) 266-121

C **In Kavála:**

Great Britain and Eire. Thessaloníkis 45; tel. (051) 223-704.

CONVERTER CHARTS. For fluid and distance measures, see page 110. Greece uses the metric system.

Temperature

Length

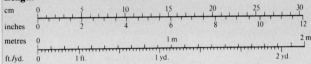

Weight

grams	0	100	200	300	400	500	600	700	800	900	1 kg
oz./lb.	0	4	8	12	1 lb	20	24	28	2 lb.		

COURTESIES. See also MEETING PEOPLE. Northern Greece is proud of its growing tourist industry, and people go out of their way to be helpful to visitors. If you ask for directions in Salonica, for example, your informant will often accompany you to your destination. Most Greeks are more than happy to cooperate in making your photography a success and will pose willingly. The smallest effort to speak a few words of Greek will be greatly appreciated.

Social conventions are quite strictly observed. A handshake is normal when meeting and parting from a friend. Shopkeepers expect a "good morning" (or "good afternoon") and a "goodbye" (see LANGUAGE).

Greeks, in common with most continental Europeans, wish each other "bon appétit" before a meal. In Greek, the expression is *kalí órexi*. A common toast when drinking is *stin igiá sas*, meaning "cheers". A reply to any toast, *epísis*, means "the same to you". It is not considered good manners to fill a wine glass nor to drain it completely. The custom is to keep it topped up.

Don't show the palms of your hands when waving. This gesture is known as *moúntza* and considered offensive, especially in out-of-the-way places. Learn to wave in regal fashion with the palm towards you.

CRIME and THEFT. Honesty is a matter of pride. Any idea of stealing from a guest is thoroughly repellent to this hospitable nation. Nevertheless, common sense suggests you keep an eye on things and confide valuable jewellery to the hotel reception.

You should keep in mind that possession of narcotics is a serious matter in Greece.

DRIVING IN GREECE

D

Entering Greece: To bring your car into Greece you'll need:

- International Driving Permit (see below)
- Car registration papers
- Insurance coverage (the Green Card is no longer obligatory within the EEC, but comprehensive coverage is advisable)
- Nationality plate or sticker

The International Driving Permit (not required for holders of a British licence) can be obtained through your home motoring association or through the Greek Automobile and Touring Club (ELPA) on presentation of your national licence, your passport and two photographs. A small fee is charged.

If you don't have a Green Card, you'll be required to take out Greek insurance at your point of entry.

The standard European red warning triangle is required in Greece for emergencies. Seat belts are obligatory. Motorcycle riders and their passengers must wear crash helmets.

Speed limits are 100 kilometres per hour (62 m.p.h.) on motorways (expressways), 80 k.p.h. (50 m.p.h.) on country roads and 50 k.p.h. (31 m.p.h.) in towns.

Driving conditions. All major roads in Northern Greece are asphalted and generally of the straight and undulating variety, owing to the nature of the countryside. You will, however, encounter winding roads in the mountainous Cholomón region, but the surfaces are good.

All roads leading from Salonica to the playgrounds of the three Halkidiki peninsulas are well-constructed. Traffic is heavy at peak periods and always fast in open country. A Greek behind the wheel is a formidable fellow. Tractors and herds of goats add to the hazards.

The road from Stratóni to Stavrós on the east coast of the Halkidiki mainland appears from maps to be a quick 33-kilometre dash. Note, however, that this is a first-gear situation even for four-wheel drive vehicles.

D Thásos is graced with a road exceptional for a small island, and you can ship your car and caravan (trailer) there.

On Samothrace, stick to local taxis in developed areas, and horses or ponies in the mountain regions. These fine-boned little animals are sure-footed when the road runs out.

Parking. In town centres, the number plates of all cars badly or illegally parked are removed by the authorities. Not only is getting them back an expensive process, you also may have to wait up to ten days. The best way to ruin a holiday, in fact.

Traffic police (see also under POLICE) keep a strict eye out for speeding and double overtaking, especially on Kassándra peninsula.

Fuel and Oil. While service stations are plentiful in Northern Greece, the supply of petrol (gasoline) may be less than adequate. You could meet with a shake of the head or up-cast eyes which, interpreted, means "sorry, no gas". Fill up wherever possible, even if the tank is registering half-full. Note that the majority of service stations close at 7 p.m. or earlier (especially at weekends). Be careful, because only a few stay open in turns after that hour. You can get normal-grade petrol (90 octane), super (98) and diesel.

Fluid measures

imp. gals. 0 — 5 — 10

litres 0 5 10 20 30 40 50

U.S. gals. 0 — 5 — 10

Distances. Here are some approximate road distances in kilometres between Salonica and some major centres:

Alexandroúpolis	340	Kavála	165
Athens	510	Komotiní	275
Dráma	165	Orestiáda	455
Flórina	160	Polígiros	70

To convert kilometres to miles:

km 0 1 2 3 4 5 6 8 10 12 14 16

miles 0 ½ 1 1½ 2 3 4 5 6 7 8 9 10

Breakdowns. The ELPA Road Assistance Service in Salonica covers a radius of 60 kilometres from town. Dial 104. The motorway Patras – Athens – Salonica– Évzoni (near the Yugoslav frontier) is patrolled by

ELPA vehicles bearing the sign "O. V. E. L. P. A."/"Assistance Routière A. T. C. C."/"Road Assistance".

ELPA's address in Salonica:
Vas. Ólgas 228; tel. (031) 426-319

Road signs: Most road signs are the standard pictographs used throughout Europe. However, you may encounter these written signs:

ΑΔΙΕΞΟΔΟΣ	No through road
ΑΛΤ	Stop
ΑΝΩΜΑΛΙΑ ΟΔΟΣΤΡΩΜΑΤΟΣ	Bad road surface
ΑΠΑΓΟΡΕΥΕΤΑΙ Η ΑΝΑΜΟΝΗ	No waiting
ΑΠΑΓΟΡΕΥΕΤΑΙ Η ΕΙΣΟΔΟΣ	No entry
ΑΠΑΓΟΡΕΥΕΤΑΙ Η ΣΤΑΘΜΕΥΣΙΣ	No parking
ΔΙΑΒΑΣΙΣ ΠΕΖΩΝ	Pedestrian crossing
ΕΛΑΤΤΩΣΑΤΕ ΤΑΧΥΤΗΤΑΝ	Reduce speed
ΕΠΙΚΙΝΔΥΝΟΣ ΚΑΤΩΦΕΡΕΙΑ	Dangerous incline
ΕΡΓΑ ΕΠΙ ΤΗΣ ΟΔΟΥ	Roadworks in progress (Men working)
ΚΙΝΔΥΝΟΣ	Caution
ΜΟΝΟΔΡΟΜΟΣ	One-way traffic
ΠΑΡΑΚΑΜΠΤΗΡΙΟΣ	Diversion (Detour)
ΠΟΔΗΛΑΤΑΙ	Cyclists
ΠΟΡΕΙΑ ΥΠΟΧΡΕΩΤΙΚΗ ΔΕΞΙΑ	Keep right

(International) Driving Licence	**(diethnís) ádia odigíseos**
car registration papers	**ádia kikloforías**
Green Card	**asfália aftokinítou**
Can I park here?	**Boró na stathméfso edó?**
Are we on the right road for…?	**Ímaste sto sostó drómo giá…?**
Full tank, please—	**Na to gemísete me venzíni**
normal/super.	**aplí/soúper, parakaló.**
Check the oil/tires/battery.	**Na elénxete ta ládia/ta lásticha/ ti bataría.**
I've had a breakdown.	**Épatha mía vlávi.**
There's been an accident.	**Égine éna distíchima.**

ELECTRIC CURRENT. The standard current is 220-volt, 50-cycle A. C. Sockets are either two- or three-pin. Larger hotels are often able to supply plug adaptors.

I need an adaptor/a battery, please.	**Chriázome éna metaschimatistí/ mía bataría, parakaló.**

E **EMERGENCIES.** The following numbers are the ones to call in case of emergency.

Police emergency squad	100
Fire	199

Depending on the nature of the emergency, refer also to the separate entries in this section such as CONSULATES, MEDICAL CARE, POLICE.

These words are handy to know in difficult situations:

ENTRY and CUSTOMS REGULATIONS. See also DRIVING. Visitors from EEC (Common Market) countries only need an identity card to enter Greece. Citizens of most other countries must be in possession of a valid passport. European and North American residents are not subject to any health requirements. In case of doubt, check with Greek representatives in your own country before departure.

The following chart shows the quantities of certain major items you may take into Greece and, upon your return home, into your own country:

Into:	Cigarettes		Cigars		Tobacco	Spirits		Wine
Greece 1)	300	or	75	or	400 g.	1½ l.	and	5 l.
2)	200	or	50	or	250 g.	1 l.	or	2 l.
3)	400	or	100	or	500 g.	see 1) and 2)		
Australia	200	or	200 g. or		250 g.	1 l.	or	1 l.
Canada	200	and	50	and	900 g.	1.1 l.	or	1.1 l.
Eire	200	or	50	or	250 g.	1 l.	and	2 l.
N. Zealand	200	or	50	or	250 g.	1.1 l.	and	4.5 l.
S. Africa	400	and	50	and	250 g.	1 l.	and	2 l.
U.K.	200	or	50	or	250 g.	1 l.	and	2 l.
U.S.A.	200	and	100	and	4)	1 l.	or	1 l.

1) Residents of Europe, non-duty-free items purchased in EEC countries (alcoholic-beverage allowances—also for non European residents)
2) Residents of Europe, items purchased outside EEC countries or in EEC countries duty-free (alcoholic beverage allowances—also for non-European residents)
3) Residents outside Europe
4) A reasonable quantity

Currency restrictions. As a visitor, you may take into or out of the country a maximum of 3,000 drachmas in banknotes of up to 500 drachmas. There's no limit on the foreign currency or traveller's cheques you may import or export as a tourist, though amounts in excess of $500 or its equivalent must be declared to the customs official upon arrival.

I've nothing to declare.	**Den écho na dilóso típota.**
It's for my personal use.	**Íne giá prosopikí chrísi.**

GUIDES and INTERPRETERS *(xenagós; dierminéas).* Guides from tour agencies accompany groups to the main archaeological sites. They speak several major European languages. If you want a personal guide you should enquire at the tourist office or at a tour agency.

Interpreters for conferences and business discussions are highly trained professionals. Enquire at your consulate.

We'd like an English-speaking guide.	**Tha thélame éna xenagó na milá i angliká.**
I need an English interpreter.	**Chriázome éna ánglo dierminéa.**

HAIRDRESSERS (ΚΟΜΜΩΤΗΡΙΟ—*kommotírio*) **and BARBERS** (ΚΟΥΡΕΙΟ—*kourío*). You can expect intense and genuine personal interest not only in your hair, but also in yourself. Hairdressers are delightfully friendly, but don't expect them to be fast.

Major beach hotels often have hairdressing facilities. Enquire at the reception desk.

Tip 10–15%.

The following vocabulary will help:

I'd like a shampoo and set.	**Thélo loúsimo ke miz-an-plí.**
I want a...	**Thélo...**
haircut	**koúrema**
blow-dry (brushing)	**chténisma me to pistoláki**
permanent wave	**permanád**
colour chart	**éna digmatológio**
colour rinse	**mía dekolorasión**
manicure	**manikioúr**
Don't cut it too short.	**Mi ta kópsete kondá.**
A little more off (here).	**Lígo pió kondá (edó).**

113

H **HITCH-HIKING** (*oto-stóp*). In a country where human contact is valued, it is considered perfectly normal to give a lift, or to ask for one.

Can you give me/us a lift to…?	**Boríte na me/mas páte méchri to…?**

HOTELS and ACCOMMODATION* (ΞΕΝΟΔΟΧΕΙΟ; ΔΩΜΑΤΙΑ— *xenodochío; domátia*). See also CAMPING and YOUTH HOSTELS. In 1965 there were 615 overnight stays in all of Halkidiki. In 1977 there were 3,838,084 and numbers have increased since. This gives some indication of the development of the area.

Accommodation ranges from super luxury-class hotel-bungalows to modest rooms in private houses.

If you arrive without reserving, contact the EOT tourist reception desk at Salonica Airport or call at the EOT office in the city (see TOURIST INFORMATION OFFICES). The local tourist police will also advise on accommodation throughout the area.

I'd like a single/double room.	**Tha íthela éna monó/dipló domátio.**
with bath/shower	**me bánio/dous**
What's the rate per night?	**Piá íne i timí giá mía níkta?**

L **LANGUAGE.** See also ALPHABET and box on page 24. Some people have worked in Germany, Australia or the United States and speak German or English. Some speak French. Nevertheless you'll often meet Greeks who speak nothing but their own language. The Berlitz phrase book GREEK FOR TRAVELLERS covers practically all the situations you are likely to encounter.

The Greeks themselves actually have two languages—the classical *katharévousa*, until recently the language of the courts and parliament and still used by a few conservative newspapers, and *dimotikí*, the spoken language and now also the official one. This is what you'll hear in Greece today.

The following phrases are ones you'll want to use often:

Good morning	**Kaliméra**	Please	**Parakaló**
Good afternoon	**Kalispéra**	Thank you	**Efcharistó**
Good night	**Kaliníkta**	Goodbye	**Chérete**

Do you speak English?	**Miláte angliká?**
I don't speak Greek.	**Den miló elliniká.**

LAUNDRY and DRY-CLEANING (ΠΛΥΝΤΗΡΙΟ—*plintírio;* ΚΑΘΑ-ΡΙΣΤΗΡΙΟ—*katharistírio*). In this climate it's easy to rinse out small articles yourself. They dry in just a few hours.

During the peak season, allow three or four days for hotel laundry and dry-cleaning services. You'll find it quicker and cheaper to go to the local laundry, but colours may come back faded.

Where's the nearest laundry/ dry-cleaners?	**Pou íne to kodinótero plintírio/ katharistírio?**
When will it be ready?	**Póte tha íne étimo?**
I must have this for tomorrow morning.	**Prépi na íne étimo ávrio to proí.**

LOST PROPERTY. If you lose something, you have a good chance of getting it back—the Greek reputation for honesty is well merited. While there aren't lost property offices in Northern Greece, in all likelihood anything lost will be turned in to the local police station, or kept in the place where you left it. Otherwise contact the local tourist police.

I've lost my wallet/handbag/ passport.	**Échasa to portofóli mou/ti tsánda mou/to diavatirió mou.**

MAPS. The National Tourist Organization (EOT) provide simplified, accurate maps of various parts of the region in their tourist brochures, with street- and place-names given in the Roman alphabet. These are also available at most hotel reception desks. The maps in this book are by Falk-Verlag, Hamburg.

I'd like a street plan of…	**Tha íthela éna odikó chárti tou…**
a road map of this region	**éna chárti aftís tis periochís**

MEDICAL CARE. It is sensible to take out health insurance covering the risk of illness or accident while you're on holiday. Your insurance representative or travel agent at home will be able to advise. On the spot, you can turn to a Greek insurance company for coverage corresponding to your requirements and length of stay. Emergency treat-

M ment is free, but with insurance coverage you'll enjoy better medical care in case of hospitalization.

The two main tourist complaints are sunburn and stomach upsets. Moderation in eating and drinking should see you over the change of diet. Go easy on the olive oil and wine, and don't let too much sun spoil your holiday and your tan. Treat yourself to a good pair of sunglasses, and avoid the heat between 11 a.m. and 2 p.m.

Pharmacies (ΦΑΡΜΑΚΕΙΟ—*farmakío*) are easily recognized by the sign outside—a red cross on a white background. Chemists take turns in offering a 24-hour service in Salonica. The address of the chemist on duty will be posted on all pharmacy doors.

Pharmacists can generally advise on minor problems such as cuts, sunburn, blisters, throat infections and gastric disorders.

Where's the nearest (all-night) pharmacy?	**Pou íne to kodinótero (dianikterévon) farmakío?**
I need a doctor/dentist.	**Chriázome éna giatró/odontogiatró.**
an ambulance	**éna asthenofóro**
hospital	**nosokomío**
sunburn	**éngavma apó ton ílio**
sunstroke	**ilíasi**
a fever	**piretós**
an upset stomach	**varistomachiá**

MEETING PEOPLE. Salonica has a big-city atmosphere, but people have remained friendly and helpful. Visitors are always treated with an old-fashioned, courteous formality. The local gathering place is Platía Aristotélous, where cafés offer evening aperitifs and late-night snacks. You'll see people of all ages here; one of the appealing things about Greece is this mingling of the generations.

It's easy to make friends of all ages on the beaches. Incidentally, a tradition exists for getting to know foreigners who aren't sun-tanned, since they have obviously just arrived and are likely to be around for a while. The sun-tanned ones, on the other hand, are probably about to pack their bags!

How do you do?	**Ti kánete?**
How are you?	**Pos íste?**
Very well, thank you.	**Polí kalá, efcharistó.**

MONEY MATTERS

Currency. Greece's monetary unit is the drachma (*drachmí*, abbreviated drs.—in Greek, Δρχ.).

Coins: 1, 2, 5, 10, 20, 50, drachmas.
Banknotes: 50, 100, 500, 1,000, 5,000 drachmas.
For currency restrictions, see CUSTOMS AND ENTRY REGULATIONS.

Banking hours. Hours of operation vary slightly, but in general banks (ΤΡΑΠΕΖΑ—*trápeza*) are open:

8.30 a.m. to 2 p.m., Monday to Thursday, till 1.30 p.m. on Fridays.

In Salonica, the National Bank of Greece at Tsimiskí 11 is open:

8.30 a.m. to 2 p.m. and, for foreign exchange, 5.30 to 8 p.m., Monday to Friday, and 8.30 a.m. to 2 p.m. on Saturdays and Sundays, for foreign exchange.

Major hotels change money, but at a slightly less advantageous rate than banks. Take your passport as identification.

Credit Cards and Traveller's Cheques (*pistotikí kárta; "traveller's cheque"*). Internationally known credit cards are honoured in most shops (indicated by a sign in the window) and by all banks, car hire firms and leading hotels. Traveller's cheques, widely accepted, are best cashed at a bank (remember your passport for identification).

Paying cash. You may be able to pay for goods in some places with foreign currency, but paying in drachmas is less trouble for everybody.

I want to change some pounds/ dollars.	**Thélo na alláxo merikés líres/ meriká dollária.**
Do you accept traveller's cheques?	**Pérnete "traveller's cheques"?**
Can I pay with this credit card?	**Boró na plclose me aftí ti pistotikí kárta?**

NEWSPAPERS and MAGAZINES *(efimerída; periodikó).* Most foreign dailies—including the principal British newspapers and the Paris-based *International Herald Tribune*—appear on news-stands the day following publication. There is a good selection of foreign magazines from most European countries.

Have you any English-language newspapers?	**Échete anglikés efimerídes?**

P **PHOTOGRAPHY.** A photo shop is advertised by the sign ΦΩΤΟΓ-ΡΑΦΕΙΟ *(fotografío)*. Leading brands of film are usually available in Salonica. There are no Greek makes. Black-and-white film is processed in a couple of days, but colour slides and colour film will take one to two weeks. Hand-held cameras may be used in some, but not all, museums and at archaeological sites. The complicated restrictions on use of tripods and cine-filming are not always strictly applied. For security reasons it is illegal to use a tele-photo lens aboard an aircraft. Military sites are, of course, taboo for cameras and are always marked accordingly.

I'd like some film for this camera.	**Tha íthela éna film giaftí ti michaní.**
black-and-white film	**asprómavro film**
colour prints	**énchromo film**
colour slides	**énchromo film giá sláids**
35-mm film	**éna film triánda pénde milimétr**
super-8	**soúper-októ**
How long will it take to develop (and print) this film?	**Se póses iméres boríte na emfanísete (ke na ektipósete) aftó to film?**
May I take a picture?	**Boró na páro mía fotografía?**

POLICE *(astinomía)*. Regular policemen are called *chorofílakes*. You'll recognize them by their grey-green uniforms.

The tourist police *(touristikí astinomía)* are a separate branch of the police force whose job it is to help foreign visitors in distress. The national flag emblems sewn on their grey uniforms indicate which foreign languages they speak. The Salonica tourist police headquarters is at Egnatías 10 (tel. [031] 522-587/9).

There are also permanent tourist police stations in:

Alexandroúpolis, Karaiskáki 6.
Kastoriá, Grámmou 24.
Kavála, Omonías 91.
Thásos (tourist season only), tel. (0593) 221-500.

Where's the nearest police station?	**Pou íne to kodinótero astinomikó tmíma?**

PUBLIC HOLIDAYS *(argíes)*. Banks, offices and shops are closed
throughout Greece on the following civil and religious holidays:

Jan. 1	*Protochroniá*	New Year's Day
Jan. 6	*ton Theofanion*	Epiphany
March 25	*Ikostí Pémti Martíou (tou Evangelismoú)*	Greek Independence Day
May 1	*Protomagiá*	May Day
Aug. 15	*Dekapendávgoustos (tis Panagías)*	Assumption Day
Oct. 28	*Ikostí Ogdói Oktovríou*	*Óchi* ("No") Day, commemorating Greek defiance of Italian ultimatum and invasion of 1940
Dec. 25	*Christoúgenna*	Christmas Day
Dec. 26	*défteri iméra ton Christougénnon*	St. Stephen's Day
Movable dates:	*Katharí Deftéra*	1st Day of Lent: Clean Monday
	Megáli Paraskeví	Good Friday
	Deftéra tou Páscha	Easter Monday
	Análipsis	Ascension

Note: The dates on which the movable holy days are celebrated often differ from those in the West.

Are you open tomorrow? **Échete aniktá ávrio?**

RADIO and TV *(rádio; tileórasi).* The Greek National Radio (ERT) broadcasts the news and weather in English in the morning, afternoon and evening.

On short-wave bands, reception of the World Service of the BBC is extremely clear. Voice of America's English programmes are also easily picked up.

Most hotels, and some bars and restaurants have TV lounges. Many of the programmes are well-known TV series in English with Greek subtitles.

RELIGIOUS SERVICES *(litourgía).* The national church is the Greek Orthodox. In Salonica, visitors of certain other faiths will be able to attend services (in Greek only) at the following places of worship:

R **Catholic.** Frángon 39; tel. (031) 539-550. Sunday at 8 and 10 a.m. and 6 p.m., Monday to Saturday at 8 a.m.

Protestant. Konstantínou Paleológou 6; tel. (031) 273-380. Sunday at 10.30 a.m. and 7 p.m. Bible Study Thursday at 8.30 p.m.

Jewish. Tsimiskí 24 (the Jewish Club), daily.

Is there a Catholic church/ Protestant church/synagogue near here?	**Ipárchi mía katholikí eklisía/ eklisía diamartiroménon/sinagogí edó kondá?**
What time is mass/the service?	**Ti óra archízi i litourgía?**

S **SIESTA.** Greece's entry into the Common Market may mean the abandonment of this sensible Mediterranean habit. But as of now, Salonica is pretty much a deserted city between 1.30 and 4 or 5 p.m.

SIGHTSEEING TOURS. Agencies organize guided tours from both Salonica and Kavála, as well as from Halkidiki hotels. In Salonica, you can join a 2½-hour sightseeing tour around the town, or a 3-hour afternoon trip to Pélla, birthplace of Alexander the Great. There are also full-day excursions to Pélla and Kavála, as well as to Mount Áthos *(Ágion Óros)* and various other sites on the Halkidiki peninsula. Two-day tours cover the monasteries of Metéora. Check with your hotel receptionist or a travel agency for further details, or contact the tourist information office.

Admission to Mount Áthos is strictly controlled and all prospective independent visitors must obtain residence permits. (Tour agencies make the necessary arrangements for members of organized excursion groups.) You will be granted the right to one on presentation of a letter of introduction from your embassy or consulate to the Greek Ministry of Foreign Affairs in Athens or the Ministry of Northern Greece in Salonica (see below).

Women are not admitted; nor (except for theology students) are men under 21. Passport control takes place at Dáfni; you then proceed to Káries, capital of the Áthos community, where your residence permit is issued. The usual length of stay is four days.

Travel from one monastery to another is usually on foot, so it is essential to travel light. You will be asked to present your permit to the guest master at each stop.

Greek Ministry of Foreign Affairs (Directorate of Churches): Zalokósta 2, Athens; tel. (01) 3626-894.

Ministry of Northern Greece (Directorate of Civic Affairs): Platía Diikitiríou, Salonica; tel. (031) 270-092.

SPORTS CLUBS and CENTRES

Basketball. Byzantine Athletic Club, Koúskoura 7, Salonica; tel. (031) 270-379.

Mountain Climbing. Contact the Greek Skiing and Alpine Association, Karólou Dil 19, Salonica; tel. (031) 278-288.

Riding. Northern Greece Riding Club, Mikró Émvolo (suburb of Salonica); tel. (031) 416-895.

Ktíma Lítsa Riding Centre, near Thérmi; tel. (031) 461-204.

Rowing and Sailing. Kalamariá Naval Club, Néa Kríni, Salonica; tel. (031) 412-068.

Alexandroúpolis Naval Club, Alexandroúpolis; tel. (0551) 28-577.

Skiing, see "Mountain Climbing" above.

Swimming and Diving Lessons are given at the Poseidon Sports and Athletic Centre, at the end of Leofóros Megálou Alexándrou in Salonica.

Tennis. The Athletic Centre above has courts where anyone can play; non-members are also admitted at the Thessaloníki Tennis Club, Kíprou 16, Vizántio, Salonica.

Water-ski training centres. Thessaloníki Sailing Club, Leofóros Megálou Alexándrou, Salonica; tel. (031) 830-939.

Gerakína Beach Hotel, Gerakíni, Halkidiki; tel. (0371) 22-474.

Áthos Palace/Pallíni hotels, Kalithéa, Kassándra, Halkidiki; tel. (0374) 22-100 / 22-480.

TIME DIFFERENCES. The chart below shows the time difference between Greece and various cities in winter. In summer, Greek clocks are put forward one hour.

New York	London	**Greece**	Johannesburg	Sydney	Auckland
5 a.m.	10 a.m.	**noon**	noon	9 p.m.	11 p.m.

What time is it?   **Ti óra íne?**

T **TIPPING.** By law, service charges are included in the bill at hotels, restaurants and *tavérnes*. Whether you leave a tip or not depends on the service you received and whether someone went out of his or her way to be personally helpful. A tip, after all, is a gift, and you will encounter no unpleasantness if you don't give one.

Hotel porter, per bag	30–50 drs.
Maid, per day	100 drs.
Waiter	5% (optional)
Taxi driver	10% (optional)
Tour guide	100–200 drs. (optional)
Hairdresser/Barber	10%
Lavatory attendant	20 drs.

TOILETS (ΤΟΥΑΛΕΤΤΕΣ—*toualéttes*). In Salonica, there are public toilets on the seaward side of the White Tower and in Platía Aristotélous. The usual picture symbols on the doors indicate "men's" and "women's", or the Greek words may be used, ΓΥΝΑΙΚΩΝ (ladies) and ΑΝΔΡΩΝ (gentlemen).

Where are the toilets? **Pou íne i toualéttes?**

TOURIST INFORMATION OFFICES (*grafío pliroforión tourismoú*). The National Tourist Organization staff will do all they can to aid you, both in preparing for your trip and while you're in Greece. They supply a wide range of accurate, colourful brochures and maps for the region in various languages and advise on hotel prices and addresses, campsites and itineraries.

Australia. 51–57 Pitt St., Sydney, N.S.W. 2000; tel. (02) 241-1663.

British Isles. 195–7, Regent St., London W1R 8DL; tel. (01) 734-5997.

Canada. 80 Bloor St. West, Suite 1403, Toronto, Ont. M5S 2Vl; tel. (416) 968-2220.
1233 rue de la Montagne, Montreal, Que. H3G 1Z2; tel (514)
122 871-1532.

U.S.A. 645 5th Ave., New York, NY 10022; tel (212) 421-5777;
611 W. 6th St., Los Angeles, CA 90017; tel. (213) 626-6696;
168 N. Michigan Ave., Chicago, IL 60601; tel. (312) 782-1084;
Building 31, State St., Boston, MA 02109; tel. (617) 227-7366.

The central headquarters of the National Tourist Organization of
Greece (NTOG), or Ellinikós Organismós Tourismoú (EOT), is in
Athens, at Amerikís 2 (tel. [01] 3223-111/9).

In **Salonica,** the EOT office is at Platía Aristotélous 8 (tel. [031] 222-935/271-888).

There is also a desk at Salonica Airport, tel. (031) 425-011, ext. 215.

Kavála has an EOT office at Philellínon 2 (tel. [051] 228-762).

Where's the tourist office? **Pou íne to grafío tourismoú?**

TRANSPORT

Boat services. Car ferries link the islands of Samothrace and Thásos to
the mainland:

Kavála—Thásos: 7 boats daily, 1½-hour trip.

Keramotí—Thásos: 7 boats daily, 45-minute trip.

Alexandroúpolis—Samothrace: 1 boat daily, 2½-hour trip.

Bus services. Vehicles in Northern Greece may not look attractive,
but don't be deceived by appearances; all are reliable, reasonably
frequent and punctual.

In Salonica, rush-hour buses are to be avoided. An all-night city
service operates, but after midnight it functions only at long intervals.

You enter buses from the rear, buying your ticket when on board.
Keep your ticket; it might be asked for.

In summer, some 15 buses link Salonica daily with Athens, a trip of
7½ to 8 hours.

The bus for Halkidiki leaves from Karakási 68 in Salonica.

ΣΤΑΣΙΣ *(stásis)* is the bus-stop sign.

Taxis★, plentiful, cheap and convenient, provide a good means of
transport throughout Northern Greece. Drivers don't try to cheat passengers, so round off the fare, and even give a bit more, say 10%.
Small extra charges are added for luggage, late-night service, waiting
and over special holidays.

T In Salonica, taxis are blue and white with a taxi (ΤΑΞΙ) sign on the roof. Use them to visit the major tourist sights, avoiding rush hours. You can hail a taxi in the street or queue at a rank.

Trains. Rail services link Salonica with Athens (six trains daily) and towns in Macedonia and Thrace. Information should be sought from the Railways Organization (OSE) at:
Aristotélous 18–20 in Salonica or from the city's new rail terminal at Monastiríou.

In Athens, trains for Salonica leave from the major international station, Stathmós Larísis.

Where's the railway station/ the nearest bus stop?	**Pou íne o sidirodromikós stathmós/o kodinóteros stathmós ton leoforíon?**
When's the next boat/bus/ train to…	**Póte févgi to epómeno plío/leoforío/tréno giá…?**
I want a ticket to…	**Thélo éna isitírio giá…**
single (one-way)	**apló**
return (round-trip)	**me epistrofí**
first/second class	**próti/deftéra thési**
Will you tell me when to get off?	**Tha mou píte pou na katevó?**
Where can I get a taxi?	**Pou boró na vro éna taxí?**
What's the fare to…?	**Piá íne i timí giá…?**

W **WATER** *(neró).* Tap water is safe to drink. Bottled mineral water is also available.

a bottle of mineral water	**éna boukáli metallikó neró**
fizzy (carbonated)/still	**me/chorís anthrakikó**

Y **YOUTH HOSTELS** (ΞΕΝΩΝ ΝΕΟΤΗΤΟΣ—*xenón neótitos*). Admission to youth hostels in Greece is reserved for those possessing an international membership card, and maximum stay is ten days.

In Salonica, there is one YMCA (ΧΑΝ) and one YWCA (ΧΕΝ):
YMCA: Platía X.A.N.T.H., tel. (031) 275-026.
124 YWCA: Agías Sofías 11, tel. (031) 276-144/5.

SOME USEFUL EXPRESSIONS

yes/no	**ne/óchi**
please/thank you	**parakaló/efcharistó**
excuse me/you're welcome	**me sinchoríte/típota**
where/when/how	**pou/póte/pos**
how long/how far	**póso keró/póso makriá**
yesterday/today/tomorrow	**chthes/símera/ávrio**
day/week/month/year	**iméra/evdomáda/mínas/ chrónos**
left/right	**aristerá/dexiá**
up/down	**epáno/káto**
good/bad	**kalós/kakós**
big/small	**megálos/mikrós**
cheap/expensive	**ftinós/akrivós**
hot/cold	**zestós/kríos**
old/new	**paliós/néos**
open/closed	**aniktós/klistós**
here/there	**edó/ekí**
free (vacant)/occupied	**eléftheri/kratiméni**
early/late	**norís/argá**
easy/difficult	**éfkolos/dískolos**
Does anybody here speak English?	**Milá kanís angliká?**
What does this mean?	**Ti siméni aftó?**
I don't understand.	**Den katalavéno.**
Please write it down.	**Parakaló grápste to.**
Is there an admission charge?	**Prépi na pliróso ísodo?**
Waiter, please!	**Parakaló!**
I'd like…	**Tha íthela…**
How much is that?	**Póso káni aftó?**
Have you something less expensive?	**Échete káti ftinótero?**
What time is it?	**Ti óra íne?**
Just a minute.	**Éna leptó.**
Help me, please.	**Voithíste me, parakaló.**

Index

An asterisk (*) next to a page number indicates a map reference. Where place names are written in their Greek form on the maps, they are given in brackets behind the English name.

For an index to Practical Information, see page 101.

INDEX

INDEX

128

BERLITZ PHRASE BOOKS

World's bestselling phrase books feature not only expressions and vocabulary you'll need, but also travel tips, useful facts and pronunciation throughout. The handiest and most readable conversation aid available.

Arabic	French	Portuguese
Chinese	German	Russian
Danish	Greek	Serbo-Croatian
Dutch	Hebrew	Spanish
European (14 languages)	Hungarian	Latin-American Spanish
	Italian	
European Menu Reader	Japanese	Swahili
	Norwegian	Swedish
Finnish	Polish	Turkish

BERLITZ CASSETTEPAKS

The above-mentioned titles are also available combined with a cassette to help you improve your accent. A helpful 32-page script is included containing the complete text of the dual language hi-fi recording.

TRAVEL WITH BERLITZ!

ISBN 1-85238-067-5

£2.95

Letts ®

9 781852 380670

BULGARIA

YUGOSLAVIA

Limni
Prespa

Kavála   Alexandroúpolis

THESSALONÍKI

TURKEY

ALBANIA   Kastoriá   Véria   Thásos

Chalkidikí   Samothráki

Katerini   Áthos

H   Límnos

Lárisa   Vólos   E

Igoumenítsa   Skíathos   Ayvalík

Agrinion   L   Évia   Lésvos

Ág. Konstantínos   Chíos   Izmir

Pátre   L

Kórinthos   ATHÍNE   A

Míkonos   Pátmos

Spárti   Kos

Pílos   S

IONIAN SEA   AEGEAN SEA

Ródos

Kríti

Irāklion

Ἀγγλική Ἔκδοση